Linked in
UNLOCKED

GET YOUR FREE GIFT
http://LinkedInUnlockedWorkbook.com

LinkedIn Unlocked Companion Workbook provides all of the exercises, worksheets, and templates (and more) presented in this book. It's yours… **FREE to download at:** http://LinkedInUnlockedWorkbook.com

ISBN-13: 978-1987473780
This book is in no way authorized by, endorsed by, or affiliated with LinkedIn or its subsidiaries. All references to LinkedIn and other trademarked properties are used in accordance with the Fair Use Doctrine and are not meant to imply that this book is a LinkedIn product for advertising or other commercial purposes.

Bulk discounts are available to use as promotions or for corporate LinkedIn and social selling training programs. **For details email: info@topdogsocialmedia.com**

This book is also available in electronic format. Please visit **www.LinkedInUnlockedBook.com** for details.

Linked in
UNLOCKED

UNLOCK THE MYSTERY OF
LINKEDIN TO DRIVE MORE SALES
THROUGH SOCIAL SELLING

MELONIE DODARO

Praise for *LinkedIn Unlocked*

"Filled with practical advice and eye-opening tips, this is the 'user's manual' for LinkedIn you'll wish you had years ago. Highly recommended."

JAY BAER, New York Times bestselling author of
Youtility and *Hug Your Haters*

"This book covers every aspect of social selling and how you can use LinkedIn to your advantage. Don't just read this book, implement it."

JEFFREY GITOMER, New York Times bestselling author of
The Sales Bible and *The Little Red Book of Selling*

"In *LinkedIn Unlocked*, Melonie Dodaro shares her method for abandoning the old ways of selling and embracing LinkedIn as a powerful tool to generate leads that lead to sales."

MICHAEL STELZNER, CEO of Social Media Examiner,
Author of *Launch*

"Brilliant! Melonie has written a very practical, how-to course in a book. I especially love the social selling framework. I'm recommending *LinkedIn Unlocked* to all my clients!"

MARI SMITH, Premier Facebook Marketing Expert,
Author of *The New Relationship Marketing*

"In *LinkedIn Unlocked*, Melonie gives you the roadmap to activating the digital rolodex that is LinkedIn. Her practical approach to social selling will help you turn digital profiles into real-life connections and new business."

EKATERINA WALTER, Wall Street Journal bestselling author of
Think Like Zuck and *The Power of Visual Storytelling*

"It's rare that you come across a great book about LinkedIn, but Melonie has nailed it with *LinkedIn Unlocked*! Enormously helpful for anyone who wants to leverage the power of LinkedIn to achieve more leads, clients, and sales."

KIM GARST, Bestselling author of
Will the Real You Please Stand Up

"Melonie has done it again with *LinkedIn Unlocked*, providing a step-by-step process of how to combine LinkedIn with social selling, attract more clients, and add more to your bottom line."

JOEL COMM, New York Times bestselling author of
The AdSense Code and *Twitter Power 3.0*

"*LinkedIn Unlocked* could also be called Sales Unlocked! Read this book and follow Melonie's proven formula and you are guaranteed to increase sales for your business."

IAN CLEARY, Founder of RazorSocial,
Co-founder of Outreach Plus

"Responsive. Highly Pragmatic. Results Driven. A handful of words that immediately come to mind when I think of Melonie Dodaro. Her approach with *LinkedIn Unlocked* and social selling is second to none!"

REBEKAH RADICE, Founder of RadiantLA,
CMO of Post Planner

"*LinkedIn Unlocked* is a complete lead generation and revenue acceleration seminar, all in one book. Don't miss this opportunity to get inside Melonie's savvy mind for social selling and take action on what you learn in this book!

DONNA MORITZ, CEO of Socially Sorted

"If anyone can unlock the secrets, again, to utilizing LinkedIn to their advantage, it's Melonie in *LinkedIn Unlocked*. Don't miss this latest opportunity to learn from the best. Relationships are like muscle tissue, the more you engage them, the stronger and more valuable they become."

TED RUBIN, Author of *Return on Relationship* and
How to Look People in the Eye Digitally

"Melonie is spot-on! She shares the 'how to' of social selling while reinforcing it's about building relationships. If you're looking for a way to generate leads on LinkedIn, and grow in value to your network, then you must get *LinkedIn Unlocked*."

AJ WILCOX, CEO of B2Linked,
LinkedIn Advertising Consultant

"Melonie's proprietary formula outlined in *LinkedIn Unlocked*, will not only help you increase your bottom line, but it will also assist you in attracting new clients for years to come!"

ALLISON MASLAN, CEO of Pinnacle Global Network,
Author of *Blast Off* and *Scale or Fail*

"*LinkedIn Unlocked* shows you how to use LinkedIn to get directly in front of potential buyers. This is a must-read for any B2B individual, business or sales professional."

PERRY VAN BEEK, CEO of Social One,
Author of *LinkedIn Sales Navigator for Dummies*

"Concise, practical, and universally relevant. Melonie has laid out a path for you in *LinkedIn Unlocked*. Follow it!"

ANDY CRESTODINA, CMO of Orbit Media,
Author of *Content Chemistry*

"If only there were a way to make *LinkedIn Unlocked* required reading before people reached out to me on LinkedIn. That would make me happy and open the door for successful new relationships."

STEVE DOTTO,
Host of Dotto Tech

"If you want to know how to leverage LinkedIn for more business, *LinkedIn Unlocked* is a must read. This book is filled with strategies that will help you attract leads and clients, ethically."

LISA LARTER,
Bestselling author of *Pilot to Profit*

"In *LinkedIn Unlocked*, Melonie guides the reader to a 'how can I help you' mindset, which is crucial to success with modern buyers. A 'how can I help you' mindset is the only way to grow and develop relationships in today's business climate. A must-read for anyone in business."

VICTORIA TAYLOR,
Founder of Untwisted Media

"LinkedIn is one of the best tools we have at our disposal to make more sales—and there are few better at LinkedIn marketing than Melonie! If you're serious about social selling, read *LinkedIn Unlocked* asap."

LILACH BULLOCK,
Online Business Expert

"*LinkedIn Unlocked* is loaded with excellent information and is a must-read for inspired, forward-thinking professionals in search of the most effective social media methods to promote their business presence and sales revenues."

ANGUS GILLESPIE, Editor-in-Chief of
The Canadian Business Journal

"*LinkedIn Unlocked* lays out a comprehensive, yet easy-to-implement plan to make a direct impact on your lead generation and conversion goals."

LISA JENKINS,
Editor of Social Media Examiner

"Smart, engaging, and relevant. Buy the book, then put it into practice."

BRYAN KRAMER, TED Speaker and bestselling author of
Human-to-Human H2H

"Overdue and understated. *LinkedIn Unlocked* changes your thinking around social selling with a people-first approach. Melonie's modern selling techniques are well-advised, practical, and will return results that last."

JOANNE SWEENEY-BURKE,
CEO of Digital Training Institute

"When I need to up my LinkedIn game, Melonie is my go-to resource! *LinkedIn Unlocked* is a complete social selling playbook to go beyond sharing content and hoping for results, to get a measurable and consistent ROI."

EMERIC ERNOULT,
CEO of Agorapulse

"Lead generation on LinkedIn is no longer a mystery thanks to *LinkedIn Unlocked*. Melonie breaks down the exact steps to drive more sales with LinkedIn. Any business can take advantage of social selling; you just need to read this book and implement it."

SIGRUN GUDJONSDOTTIR,
Mastermind Mentor and International Speaker

"*LinkedIn Unlocked* should become your 'go to guide' for using LinkedIn to attract ideal prospects and generate sales. Don't just read it; implement what you learn and transform your business."

DYLIS GUYAN,
Sales and Marketing Leader

"In *LinkedIn Unlocked*, Melonie has once again delivered a balanced approach of sound principles and practical step-by-step advice any professional can deploy quickly. If you want to leverage LinkedIn as a business development tool, read and apply the great ideas in this book."

ED GANDIA, Host of High-Income Business Writing Podcast

"This is the roadmap to unlocking the power of LinkedIn we've all been waiting for."

HUGH CULVER, CEO BlogWorks,
Author of *Give Me a Break*

"*LinkedIn Unlocked* takes you through every step of the digital journey to reach your sales and revenue goals. The process is broken down into manageable and practical steps for anyone to achieve success."

MIC ADAM, CEO of Vanguard Leadership,
Social Selling Practitioner

"*LinkedIn Unlocked* is a remarkable tool in your social selling toolbox that gets to the heart of what matters: building real conversations and relationships, which result in increased sales."

DOYLE BUELER, CEO of Dept.Digital,
Author of *#Breakthrough*

"*LinkedIn Unlocked* is an actionable guidebook for those who want to leverage the power of LinkedIn to build their brand and their business."

PHIL GERBYSHAK, Social Selling Trainer and Speaker, Founder of The Sales Chronicles

"*LinkedIn Unlocked* is full of practical advice that can be easily implemented by anyone who is interested in building their personal brand. I've used Melonie's tips in my work with students and alumni to help them get a head start in their career."

RICHELLE MATAS, Alumni Relations at The University of British Columbia

"*LinkedIn Unlocked* completely removes the mystery of how to use LinkedIn as an effective tool for lead generation to grow your business."

SAMANTHA KELLY, Founder of Women's Inspire Network

"*LinkedIn Unlocked* shares a powerful method and structure for using LinkedIn to attract, build, and create revenue for your business. Using her powerful methods, practical ideas, and honed advice, you can lay the foundation to develop and grow lasting and authentic relationships."

ALI MEEHAN, Founder of Costa Women

"There are only a handful of people I agree with 100% when it comes to social selling on LinkedIn. Melonie Dodaro is one of them. The LINK Method™, described in detail in *LinkedIn Unlocked*, lays out the exact steps one needs to take to turn contacts into paying clients, without pitching and spamming and a clear focus on building relationships. I will recommend it to all my clients."

SARAH SANTACROCE, LinkedIn Coach and Strategist

"*LinkedIn Unlocked* articulates the power of LinkedIn and shows you exactly how to make the most of it. I'll be recommending to all my students and clients."

RENÉE VELDMAN-TENTORI,
University Lecturer, Founder of Zestee Social Media

"You have to be careful when taking advice on social selling. The approach laid out in *LinkedIn Unlocked* shows you how to have authentic communication that builds relationships. You will avoid mistakes and learn a repeatable methodology that allows you to embrace LinkedIn as a selling tool."

BETH GRANGER, LinkedIn Trainer and Consultant

"Melonie Dodaro is an expert when it comes to unraveling the mysteries of social selling through LinkedIn. In *LinkedIn Unlocked*, she shares simple but strategic steps to increase sales through the power of building relationships."

PATTY FARMER,
Marketing and Media Strategist, International Speaker

"*LinkedIn Unlocked* provides great business insights on exactly how to use LinkedIn to grow sales. It's a must-read."

SAM GOLDFARB, CEO of Tradimax

"Melonie has once again demystified LinkedIn. Her keen insights into this powerful, yet often misunderstood tool, extend well beyond mere technical applications. A must-read for anyone who wants to leverage the power of LinkedIn."

BEN ROBINSON,
Founder of Bookkeeper Business Launch

"*LinkedIn Unlocked* takes the mystery out of social selling on LinkedIn. Read it then put these techniques into action and watch your influence—and your sales—amplify!"

MELANIE BENSON,
Host of Amplify Your Success Podcast

"*LinkedIn Unlocked* is not a book; it's a code for unlocking client-getting strategies that work today, delivered in a practical, step-by-step guide."

ADAM URBANSKI, CEO of Marketing Mentors,
Author of *The Fastest Path to Cash*

"With *LinkedIn Unlocked*, you have an unfair advantage in creating valuable and profitable relationships. Follow this proven formula that will stand the test of time, regardless of any changes to social media."

SABRINA GIBSON, CEO of Social Success Academy

"Everything you need to know to use LinkedIn for business successfully, is broken down into bite-size steps in *LinkedIn Unlocked*. The book, the process, and methods are all brilliant!"

PETRA FISHER, LinkedIn Trainer and Consultant

"This book will transform—yes, transform, that's the key word there—the way you think about LinkedIn as a tool and about the whole selling process. *LinkedIn Unlocked* provides the methodology of effective social selling plus an entire step-by-step guide on how to do it."

PAUL SKAH, Author of *Brand Inside Out*,
Four times TEDx Speaker

"If generating more leads and clients is your goal, then *LinkedIn Unlocked* is the handbook. It is a must read for all sales and business development teams."

JOHN ASHCROFT,
CEO of Pro Manchester

"When I think of Melonie Dodaro, I think of her authenticity and ability to cultivate trust and genuine relationships. In *LinkedIn Unlocked*, she provides an actual strategy to drive sales in a world promising quick fixes that don't work."

LAURA TUCKER, Leadership Coach,
Host of Free Your Inner Guru™ Podcast

"Melonie has done it again with her new book *LinkedIn Unlocked*. She pulls the curtain back and reveals the true value of investing in LinkedIn for social selling."

JOHN DALE BECKLEY,
Founder of Canary PR

"If you want a predictable stream of new leads and clients from LinkedIn, then *LinkedIn Unlocked* is a must read. This book is a game changer."

JULIA BRAMBLE,
Social Media and Facebook Advertising Strategist

"*LinkedIn Unlocked* is the ultimate reference for LinkedIn marketing and lead generation! Melonie's LINK Method™ is an actionable and easy to implement plan that guarantees success."

ANTONIO CALERO,
Head of Marketing Services at AdEspresso

"*LinkedIn Unlocked* is filled with actionable tips and processes to connect with your audience and more importantly, to generate leads and more sales. It's a must-have manual for all business owners!"

IAN ANDERSON GRAY,
Founder of Seriously Social

"It's time to stop preparing to do the work and simply follow the social selling playbook laid out for you in *LinkedIn Unlocked*. It's got the Sales DNA that you need to generate more clients and sales."

PATRICK MARSHALL, TEC Canada Chair,
Business and Economic Developer

"*LinkedIn Unlocked* shows you exactly how to use LinkedIn and the art of relationship marketing to achieve real business results."

MIKE ALTON,
Brand Evangelist at Agorapulse

"Melonie Dodaro has been one of my go-to LinkedIn experts for years! *LinkedIn Unlocked* takes the reader by the hand and, not only explains how LinkedIn works, but also shows you how to shine with an actionable roadmap."

HEIDI COHEN,
Actionable Marketing Guide

CONTENTS

PREFACE

For you to achieve your desired results from this book, you'll need to not only understand the what, why, and how, but, more importantly, to be clear on the expected outcome; put what you learn into practice.

To experience results of increased sales, you will need to implement the practices and theories laid out in this book. Take the time to do the exercises and set the metrics against which you will measure the progress of your goals.

Who will benefit the most from this book?

- Sales professionals and sales leaders
- Business development managers and executives
- B2B business owners and entrepreneurs
- Vistage chairs and members
- C-Suite executives
- Professional service providers
- Coaches and consultants
- Speakers and authors
- Facilitators and trainers
- Subject matter experts and emerging thought leaders
- Digital marketing professionals
- Economic development directors

- Financial services providers

- Communications professionals

- Marketing executives

- Event managers and planners

- Business advisors

- Anyone who wants to generate leads and clients using LinkedIn!

Many others can benefit from this book. For example, I have been asked to speak at universities many times, and a recent graduate told me she was able to use this book to obtain a great new job. I've also done work with government agencies and non-profits that have significantly benefited from the principles I'm teaching.

The purpose of this book is simple. I want to help individuals and businesses successfully generate leads using LinkedIn. I'm going to share industry best practices, concept-driven exercises, and tools that have been developed from my years of experience as a professional in the social selling industry. They can be practically and immediately applied merely by reading this book and actively engaging in the exercises.

In essence, this book offers you the opportunity to implement what you read as you read it.

You will soon be growing your network, building relationships, and enhancing your personal brand and credibility. Of course, you need to commit to the work to see long-term tangible financial results.

Are you ready?

Let's get started!

Melonie Dodaro

INTRODUCTION

When you stop collecting connections and start building relationships, you increase trust and credibility; you are able to attract more clients.

Early in my life, I was a person who preferred collecting connections over building relationships. Growing up, I had never met my father. My mother, who was very young, couldn't care for me, so she left me with my grandmother. I moved often and didn't develop real relationships.

I realized that collecting connections was more convenient and safer than building meaningful relationships. If I just collected connections, I couldn't be hurt. I felt I had more control over my life, and I wouldn't be vulnerable. I had all kinds of surface level connections but lacked any real relationships.

However, knowing several people only grew the number of my acquaintances. I could never turn to an acquaintance if I needed help. Collecting acquaintances was neither productive nor helpful.

In fact, my best friend said to me once, *"Melonie, I've known you for 18 years, and I don't know anything about you."*

Her words struck me like a ton of bricks. I never realized until that day that she felt that way.

I'm a very private person. I wasn't comfortable letting people know me on a personal level. I felt strongly that business relationships were about data, and all I needed was a name and contact information. To be clear, my data-driven business models worked well, too.

At the time, I had several thriving businesses that grossed over four million dollars a year in revenue. On the surface, these businesses were thriving. But, as the market landscape changed and social selling became the norm, focusing on data and not people would have collapsed these enterprises in the future.

I would soon realize that collecting connections would be nearly worthless in the new economy of social media.

Just before selling my businesses in 2008, I reluctantly joined Facebook to stay in touch with my family that lived thousands of miles away. Shortly after, I realized it could be an effective business tool. As an entrepreneur, I look at all things from a business perspective. I joined Twitter and LinkedIn. I was convinced these platforms were going to be useful methods for marketing businesses, so I invested a lot of time and money into my education and learned all I could about social media and digital marketing.

Over time, business owners started to recognize what I was doing on various social media platforms and began asking for my help. Not long after, I started my own digital marketing company.

I quickly figured out that everyone was looking for a magic bullet that would create a significant following on social media. What they didn't realize, however, is all the followers in the world wouldn't matter if they didn't convert those into sales.

And while everyone was talking about social media, few were talking about LinkedIn. Many businesses were ignoring LinkedIn for two primary reasons:

1. It isn't sexy

2. It isn't fun or exciting

LinkedIn may not be exciting, but getting new clients and having a successful business is.

While social media is great at generating leads and connecting people, most business still takes place offline.

And that's where I saw people getting lost. They could make connections, but they couldn't build the relationships or move the conversations offline.

In fact, there are two big mistakes some people make when using LinkedIn for social selling.

They're able to keep the conversation going online, but never move it offline. It's offline that you're able to learn more about the person and their problems and ultimately convert a prospect to a client.

The other mistake some people make is that they connect with someone and rush right into pitching them and trying to sell them something. This destroys trust and any possibility of having a conversation offline.

How are you going to avoid these mistakes?

It was a long and challenging process for me. But here's what I learned—people respond to transparency and authenticity. You can't build relationships without letting people know a little bit about who you are.

Effective social selling is all about building relationships and trust.

I have developed a Social Selling Framework, which is continually evolving. However, the critical principle remains the same: the purpose is to help people move from simply collecting connections online to building relationships offline.

From this principle, I have built processes including the LinkedIn Domination Formula™ and The LINK Method™.

The LinkedIn Domination Formula™ is a proprietary formula on how to generate clients from LinkedIn. The LINK Method™ is the process to convert online connections to offline conversations. Both of these concepts can be distilled down to one foundational idea: Building Relationships and Trust.

This was all put to the test in 2015 in a way I could never have expected. One night, over dinner, a friend encouraged me to look for my father whom I had never met. This friend of mine was first an online connection, but we had developed an offline relationship. Together in a restaurant, we started searching Google, Facebook, Twitter, and LinkedIn. It was like a needle in a haystack as he had the most common Dutch name, the equivalent to John Smith in North America.

Our search came up empty.

But the thought of finding him had been planted in my mind. A week later, I opened up to another friend of mine. With her help, I shared my story in a video. Doing this involved several glasses of liquid courage (wine). I posted the video on Facebook, and over the course of a weekend, it went viral around the world through the help of my online network.

I was overwhelmed with emotion and gratitude watching this happen, but also a little bit afraid of the result.

48 hours later, it happened.

A journalist from the Netherlands, where my dad is from, contacted me through Facebook. He interviewed me, and the next day there was close to a full-page story about me in a Dutch newspaper!

My father's sister (my aunt) saw the article, and within a few hours, with a tear slightly blurring my vision, I was talking to my father for the first time in my life.

The viral craze didn't stop there.

It had become worldwide news and was covered by media in countries all around the world. I even had to choose between three American television networks that wanted to fly me overseas to meet my father in person.

Even though I was already teaching people how to use social media and LinkedIn to build relationships, I had no idea how incredibly powerful this concept was. There was more for me to learn. When you have the courage to tell your story, open up, and let people know you, they'll connect with you in a much more meaningful way.

Through my personal experience and teaching thousands of people over the years, I have weaved these ideas together into what I now teach the world. If you can learn how to move an online connection to an offline conversation, then you can go from merely collecting connections to building relationships. You'll increase trust and credibility, and you will attract more clients.

If you follow the principles in this book, never again will you say, *"I've been using LinkedIn for years, but I don't get any business from it."*

You may even experience something profound, or a miracle along the way.

This book isn't going to make new clients magically appear. That's a fairytale. What it gives you is a specific and strategic game plan to use social selling to generate more leads, qualified prospects, and clients about whom you know something.

CHAPTER ONE

DIGITAL TRANSFORMATION: SOCIAL SELLING FOR TODAY'S MODERN BUYER

LinkedIn is the premier business platform for social selling where you can find the exact group of people that makes up your target audience. What's more, this platform was designed to help you find, connect, and then build a relationship with those same people, unhindered by the gatekeepers through whom you would usually have to navigate.

But before we jump right into the details, let me ask you a few questions:

- Do you use LinkedIn for social selling?
- Do you use your LinkedIn profile to attract and communicate with potential clients?
- Do you feel good about your current online presence/personal brand?
- Do you have testimonials or recommendations (social proof) on your website and LinkedIn profile?
- Do you interact with your contacts on LinkedIn?

If your answer to any of these questions is "*NO,*" then you are doing yourself a favor by reading this book.

In this book, you will learn a step-by-step system, which takes full advantage of this online platform in as little as 30 minutes a day, helping you to increase significantly the number of leads and clients you generate. The principles and action plan I present in this book will work whether you have a free account or have invested in LinkedIn Premium or Sales Navigator.

Completing its first decade, LinkedIn boasts over half a billion global members in 200 countries[1], but it is still incorrectly viewed by many as a place to only:

- Post a resume
- Seek endorsements (a form of reference) for knowledge, skills, and abilities
- Connect with old colleagues, classmates, or friends (using the platform in the same way they use Facebook or Twitter)
- Recruit employees

Yes, you can still do all of the above with LinkedIn. However, the platform has changed a great deal over the years, and it remains the world's largest professional network.

According to a report released by LinkedIn:

- LinkedIn is the number one channel to distribute content
- LinkedIn drives more traffic to B2B blogs and sites than other social media platforms
- LinkedIn is considered the most effective social media platform for B2B lead generation
- Executives rate LinkedIn high on value gained from their social marketing initiatives

The report goes on to state:

Professionals are not just coming to LinkedIn in vast numbers; they're engaging with a huge purpose. They're coming specifically to connect to networks, brands, and opportunities by engaging with high-quality content across the LinkedIn platform. This is a very different mindset and intent from other social media platforms.

The world's professionals come to LinkedIn for:

- Industry news

- Expert advice

- Career training

- Peer insights and recommendations

- Content published by LinkedIn's influencers

While this statement indeed confirms my belief that LinkedIn is a robust social selling platform to connect with today's modern buyer, I recognize that the effort required to become a "sophisticated marketer" might appear to be an overwhelming task to those looking at this lead generation strategy for the first time. Indeed, there are still a great many people who are not using LinkedIn at all, much less to its full potential, as it can seem enormously complex.

But even the most complex of tasks can be made simple if you have a precise step-by-step system that you can replicate and follow and that will also provide you with repeatable and predictable results.

Over the years, I have created just such a lead generation system using LinkedIn. I call it the LinkedIn Domination Formula™. I will share with you exactly how and why it works. Throughout this book, I will take you through the various elements of the process I use for my private clients and show you how you can use this proven formula for your business.

I have attempted to make this book as clear and concise as possible for beginners to understand and follow, while also making sure the most advanced social sellers become even more efficient and effective with their processes.

Before jumping in and starting on this social selling journey, take a few minutes to familiarize yourself with the LinkedIn Domination Formula™ below, which will help you get a clear picture of what you can learn from this book and how it will help you become a successful modern seller.

LinkedIn Domination Formula™: Social Selling That Produces Results

If you are starting out with LinkedIn and social selling, this may seem overwhelming at first. At this stage, I'm showing the high-level overview of what I will be covering in the book and how the formula, when used as part of my step-by-step system, can help you create the results you want: more leads, more clients, and more revenue.

Each area of this formula will be discussed in detail throughout the book. You may find that the areas are not in the same order as presented in the chapters, but that's to give flexibility in doing this according to the order that makes sense to you and your business.

Figure 1.01

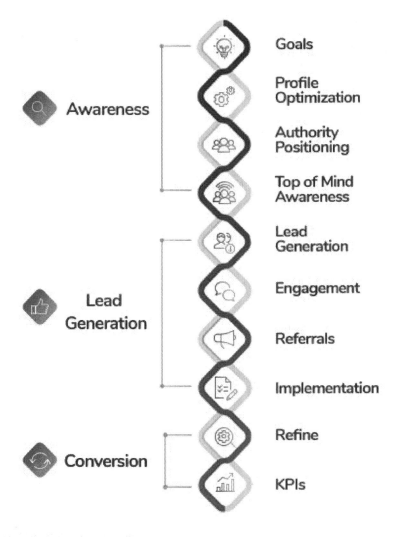

LinkedIn Domination Formula

Awareness
- Goals
- Profile Optimization
- Authority Positioning
- Top of Mind Awareness

Lead Generation
- Lead Generation
- Engagement
- Referrals
- Implementation

Conversion
- Refine
- KPIs

Stage One: Awareness

In this stage, I will show you how to stand out, get found, position yourself as an authority, and establish top of mind awareness.

Goals

You must have clearly identified goals and know your target audience.

Your goals are your map to success. Without them, you wouldn't know where to go or what steps to take. This will also help you determine your key performance indicators (KPIs). A KPI is a measurable value that demonstrates how effectively a company is achieving key business objectives. Using this metric of how much time you spend on LinkedIn each day and how many prospects you reach out to each week will give you a clear measurement of your progress.

Profile Optimization

To effectively use LinkedIn for lead generation, your LinkedIn profile must achieve three critical goals:

1. Stand out
2. Attract your ideal clients
3. Get found

Having a professional presence that's well optimized not only allows you to be found by those who are looking for someone who does what you do, but it also helps increase the success of your connection requests being accepted by decision makers. Optimizing your LinkedIn profile isn't negotiable if you want to be successful in your lead generation endeavors.

I have dedicated a later chapter to cover this subject in detail.

Authority Positioning

Content marketing along with appropriate engagement is the fastest way to position yourself as an authority and is essential to your LinkedIn lead generation success. Become a reliable source of information within your community to position yourself as a thought leader. This will boost your credibility and give potential prospects more reasons to trust you. Of course, this takes time and consistency to achieve results.

Top of Mind Awareness

Having an extensive network isn't enough if your connections forget about you after you have connected with them. Consistently sharing helpful content, both the content you create as well as that which you curate (sharing useful content from others with your commentary), will allow you to show up often and remain top of mind.

Stage Two: Lead Generation

In this stage, you will learn how to engage effectively with the right prospects, generate referrals, and move conversations offline.

Lead Generation

This is best implemented by creating a series of templated messages designed to build rapport and relationships and then ultimately move the conversation offline, where you convert a prospect to a client. Have some quality content you can use to deliver value, elicit interest, and allow you to naturally move from contact to a connection. The big mistake that many make here is they try to rush to a sale.

In a later chapter, I will show you exactly how to put this together and the approach to take for each message you send to a prospect.

Engagement

In this phase, it is crucial to pay attention to trigger events that allow for natural engagement with your ideal prospects. Effective engagement nurtures your network and provides excellent reasons for you to reach out and start a dialogue. Remember, if you don't personally engage with others, they won't engage with you.

Referrals

Mining your network of clients and those that know, like, and trust you can be one of the best sources of warm introductions. These are the clients who love you and your service and who are willing to introduce or recommend you to someone who they know could benefit from what you offer. There is tremendous value in being introduced by a trusted third-party.

Implementation

Money is in the implementation.

This is the part where you build and execute your social selling playbook. A social selling playbook is a guide for you (or your salespeople) on how you should communicate with your target audience on LinkedIn. Your playbook lists the specific tactics, activities, and messages you will use to hit your sales targets. The benefit of having a social selling playbook is that it ensures consistency and generates repeatable and predictable results.

You will find a complete chapter dedicated to precisely what your implementation plan will consist of.

Stage Three: Conversion

In this last stage, you'll see the results of your efforts and the return on investment (ROI) of your activities. Here, you can also fine-tune and modify your approach to improve your results.

Refine

It will be essential to assess the results of your social selling efforts and identify exactly how to improve those results. This is the part where you will refine your activities and messaging based on the responses you've received so far.

Key Performance Indicators

The last part of your journey to having a successful social selling system on LinkedIn is measuring your results, or KPIs. This may include reviewing the engagement you're getting from the content you're sharing, your network growth, the number of conversions, and so on. In other words, measuring what matters.

The Modern Buyer

Our world is much different than it was even just five years ago. This is because we have evolved, as have our habits, matching the evolution of our technology.

The adoption of this technology is far and wide, producing numbers[2] such as:

- Almost two-thirds of the world's population now has a mobile phone
- More than half the world now uses a smartphone
- More than half of the world's web traffic now comes from mobile phones
- More than half of all mobile connections across the globe are now "broadband"
- More than one in five of the world's population shopped online in the past 30 days

This evolution has changed the way we buy—from teenagers looking for trendy new clothes to CEOs of Fortune 500 companies looking for service solutions. In response, this has also changed the way companies sell—most notably, personalization. Big companies such as Netflix, Apple, Amazon, Google, and Facebook are all providing some personalized content online.

As the general population continues to expect more and more personalization, small- and medium-sized companies are customizing how they engage with their customers online.

The old way of selling isn't as effective with today's modern buyer. The new method of selling has evolved and requires you to educate buyers, build relationships, and connect digitally.

To increase your sales, you must understand that today's modern buyers are digitally connected at all times. They're engaged on social networks and never without a mobile phone.

Armed with this knowledge, you can gain a better understanding of what the modern buyer expects from you and through their buying process.

But there's more: how buyers respond to being sold something has changed, too. The entire sales dialogue has shifted to value-based selling.

A New Sales Dialogue: Value-Based Selling

The sales dialogue needs to shift from "What can I sell you?" to "How can I help you?"

"What can I sell you?" says:

- I care about your money.
- What else can I sell you?
- Thank you for your business.

"How can I help you?" says:

- I care about you and your business.
- How else can I add value?
- Thank you for helping us do business better.

Whether you are in North America, Europe, Australia, or anywhere else in the world, your sales dialogue must shift to "How can I help you?" if you are going to use social selling methods with any level of success.

Social Selling

Before we start laying the foundation for your social selling success, I want to make sure you fully understand what social selling (or digital sales) is and why LinkedIn is the best social media platform to use.

Defining Social Selling

Social selling refers to using social media platforms and other digital tools and processes to find and connect with potential prospects, thereby increasing sales. Social selling comes down to building relationships with potential prospects on platforms such as LinkedIn.

Social Selling = Relationship-Building

I don't think I need to tell you that the effectiveness of cold calls and emails has decreased substantially. On average, 200 emails will flood your prospect's inbox every day—most of them unwanted. 90 percent of decision makers state that they absolutely will not buy from a cold call or an unsolicited email.[3] This paints a pretty bleak outlook for any individual or company that does not embrace social selling.

While many businesses have a hard time reaching their prospects or target market using traditional marketing methods, social selling continues to grow. 75 percent of B2B buyers and 84 percent of C-level or vice-president-level executives are using social media to make purchasing decisions on platforms such as LinkedIn, where they research and exchange information on vendors and their products or services.[4] In fact, 74 percent of today's B2B buyers conduct more than half of their research online before making an offline purchase.[5]

Whether we like it or not, social selling is happening in every industry and all corners of the globe. Someone else is educating and providing insight with helpful content to your prospects and clients. Your prospects will likely take the path of least resistance and choose the company that has been helping them along their buying journey.

How will your prospects choose you over your competitors?

Data shows some powerful statistics that provide compelling evidence about the benefits of social selling. These statistics suggest that:

- Companies with formalized social selling processes are more likely to hit revenue goals. 78 percent of social sellers hit their revenue goals in the past year versus 38 percent of non-social sellers.

- Social selling gives companies higher ROI than traditional tactics do. Social sellers gain 57 percent higher ROI from social selling versus 23 percent using traditional tactics.

Your LinkedIn Quotient (LQ)

What is it and why should you care about it?

You've heard of IQ (Intelligence Quotient) and EQ (Emotional Intelligence). However, your LQ (LinkedIn Quotient) represents your knowledge of and current results with LinkedIn. Take this quick test, and it will tell you where you are in your effective use of LinkedIn. It will also indicate benefits from using it more strategically.

Each question to which you answer "Yes" will continue to improve when you implement what you learn. Each "No" will show you your missed opportunities. This book will help you maximize all opportunities, from generating leads to turning them into clients.

Let's put it to the test to understand your starting place with LinkedIn.

LINKEDIN QUOTIENT (LQ) SCALE

DIRECTIONS: Read each of the questions below and answer them by placing an X on the YES, or NO line, whichever is more relevant to the topic. Add the number of X's in the YES column to determine your current LQ.

		YES	NO
10	I have keywords in my profile that I want to be found for.	X	
9	I receive at least 100 views on each of the posts I do.		X
8	LinkedIn reports that I show up in at least 30 searches every day.		X
7	LinkedIn reports that at least 10 people view my profile every day.		X
6	My current experience is described in my profile.	X	
5	My profile is complete including past work experience, education, etc.		X
4	I receive at least 10 new connection requests each week.		X
3	My profile is written to focus on the clients I'd like to attract.	X	
2	My profile presents a comprehensive picture of who I am and what I do.	X	
1	LinkedIn has helped me generate several leads for my business.		X

Score 1 point for each X in the YES column. Write your total score here:____4____

Social Selling on LinkedIn

The most significant social selling successes to date have been achieved using LinkedIn. Statistics show it is 277 percent more effective in generating leads than either Facebook or Twitter, even though most people are not using LinkedIn to its full potential.[6]

How did it become a powerful tool for B2B social selling?

LinkedIn allows ungated access to professionals from all over the globe, as well as leaders of every Fortune 1000 company.

But who among these professionals and leaders are your ideal clients?

In the next chapter, I'll help you identify who they are and how to attract them.

CHAPTER TWO

HOW TO KNOW AND ATTRACT YOUR IDEAL CLIENTS

In the last chapter you learned that the key to successful social selling is building relationships with your prospects. We will get to that in more details; but, first, it is essential to know your target market.

To begin, ask yourself the following questions:

- Who is your ideal client (and, more specifically, who are they on LinkedIn)?

- What is the typical language of their business, industry, or organization?

- What kinds of challenges do they face?

Throughout this chapter, you'll work on a few exercises to help you answer these questions. Each exercise builds on the previous one, so take the time to complete each one in the order they are presented. From these exercises, gather the information, and use it in your LinkedIn profile, your lead generation messages, and the content you create.

Your Ideal Clients

"Everyone is not your customer."

~ Seth Godin

Steve Olsher stated, *"Profitability depends on delivering pertinent content and desired solutions to a specific audience."* When this statement and Seth Godin's quote above are taken together, a common message is revealed— one size does not fit all.

If you try to market to everyone, you market to no one.

Even though you're seeking prospects within a specific industry (where some generalities may be made), you are dealing with individuals from individual businesses. It is not the industry, company, or organization you are building a relationship with, but the individuals who make the decisions.

Begin with your ideal client in mind.

Your LinkedIn profile must be 100 percent client-focused. Show that you want to know what their problems are and that you can offer a solution. If you understand where they're coming from, what their motivations are, and if you speak their language, you'll be able to connect with them in a meaningful way.

Understanding Labels and How Your Ideal Clients Self Identify

If we asked people how they see themselves, they would probably give many different answers depending on where, when, and how we asked the question. Their description might focus on their profession, educational status, nationality, relationship status, gender, religion, recreational activities, or volunteer activities.

Often, they identify themselves with what they do, whether they're an entrepreneur, an accountant, a sales leader, a speaker, etc.

But what would you say if I asked you, *"How would you describe your-self?"* Think broadly (you can use the categories previously mentioned), and come up with as many labels as you can. Note how many of the labels are personal and how many are professional.

EXERCISE
How would you describe yourself?

You have now developed your list of labels—also referred to as egoic labels, the ones we use to describe ourselves to others. They may change over time along with changes in our professional or personal life. Nevertheless, these labels still convey what is most meaningful to us about who we are personally and what we do professionally.

For example, a woman who is also a mother will almost always identify herself first as a mother (an intrinsically and socially strong label). Some business owners might identify themselves as a business owner, while others might call themselves an entrepreneur or just describe themselves by the service they provide. Your relationship-building will fall short if you don't understand the nuances of the labels used by your prospects to identify themselves.

How Your Ideal Clients Label Themselves

For this exercise, I want you to write your answers in as much detail as you can. The goal is to know your ideal clients so well that you can think like them, speak like them, experience their emotions, and fully understand them.

I can almost hear you groan. Perhaps you think that no one would know should you decide just to skip this and the next couple of exercises and move on to the meat of the book. I can sympathize. What I am asking is difficult for most people to do. But, remember, this is essential in laying the foundation to your success in social selling. While you may not see the relevance yet, you indeed will as we go along.

Let's begin, shall we?

Think about your top 10 clients. Based on what you know about them, I would like you to identify some general commonalities and differences between them. You can sort them, for example, by role (or title), demographics, industry or organization, region served, personal traits, and leadership or management style.

> **EXERCISE**
> Describe your top 10 clients.

Narrowing your focus, I would like you to construct a list of possible labels next to each of your top 10 clients. Again, make a note of the commonalities and differences.

For example, let's say your ideal clients are technology or SaaS companies. Where are they located? Do they serve clients globally or only in a specific country? Who is the decision maker? Is it the VP of Sales? Director of Business Development? Chief Marketing Officer (CMO)?

> **EXERCISE**
> Add additional details about your top 10 clients.

Your Ideal Client's Problem/Challenge

Think about the conversations you've had with prospects and past and current clients. Answer the following questions based on the specific problem or challenge they've brought up to you.

EXERCISE

What is the specific problem they are facing?

How is that problem impacting their life, job, or business?

EXERCISE

Make a list of how that problem is impacting their life, job, or business.

What is the worst-case scenario they are facing?

EXERCISE

List some of the worst-case scenarios your ideal clients will face if they don't solve their problem.

What will they lose if they don't get that problem solved?

EXERCISE

Make a list of exactly what they will they lose if they don't solve their problem.

What has stopped them from finding a solution sooner?

EXERCISE

List some of the reasons why they have not acted on finding or implementing a solution to their problem.

Your Ideal Client's Goals and Desires

This time, let's identify the ideal solution to their problem. This is what your client hopes for the most.

What could that be?

EXERCISE

How do they describe the solution they need to solve their problem?

What will change/improve in their life, job, or business when they solve their problem?

EXERCISE

Make a list of how their life will improve when they solve their problem.

How will they feel once their problem is solved?

EXERCISE

Make a list of how they will feel and what they'll be able to do once their problem is solved.

If your ideal client could wave a magic wand and have the perfect solution to their problem, what precisely would that solution look like?

> **EXERCISE**
> The solution you think your ideal client needs and the one they'd like to see could be very different. What would the perfect solution look like to them? Go into detail here.

Your Ideal Client's Response to Your Solution

After spending some time understanding who your ideal clients are, it's time to go deeper and be even more specific. You have just provided the solution to your client's problem. What did they feel when they bought your product or service? What is going on in their mind? What did they say after their problem was solved? Are they pleased with the results because of your solution?

Write everything down that comes to mind from the perspective of your client. Write as though YOU are your ideal client, including things they may never say to you. They could be, *"I'm afraid my business will go bankrupt." "I'm afraid I will need to let go of some of my employees." "I'm afraid I'll lose my job."*

> **EXERCISE**
> What is your client thinking, saying, and feeling about their problem and the solution you provided?

It's All About the Language

Leave creativity to artists.

One big mistake sales and marketing professionals make is trying to be creative with language from their perspective rather than speaking the language of their ideal prospects and clients. Do your homework and speak their language.

Doing so will allow your message to resonate with them as you gain their trust in solving their problem for them. Let their desires be reflected in everything you do, from your LinkedIn profile to the messages you send them and the content you create and share.

Imagine you're a business coach, and you want to work with clients who are looking for ways to grow their business and make more money. You plan your approach and your marketing message to attract clients.

Which of the following questions will likely get a response?

1. Are you seeking more abundance and financial freedom?

2. Are you a business owner looking to attract more clients and make more money?

The best way to know the words and phrases your ideal clients use is to:

- Listen to the language used by your current clients

- Listen to the language used when a prospect wants to learn more about what you have to offer

- Listen to the answers to the questions asked by your prospects

Notice all three require you to listen, to really listen. Being aware of the words and phrases commonly used by your ideal clients is very important, because that is the exact language you want to include in your profile. Take notes each time you are speaking to a prospect or a client, and write down the precise language they use.

Your Why is Your Differentiator

Be clear on your why.

In addition to determining who your ideal clients are and what they need, you also need to be clear on who you are, what you stand for, and why you do what you do.

While there is probably no one who clarifies this concept as succinctly as Simon Sinek in his TED Talk, "How great leaders inspire action," which has had over 37 million views, I will attempt to explain what it is and why it is so vital to your success.

Your prospects have many options; they will choose you when they can emotionally connect with your message and why you do what you do.

If you try to speak to everyone, you will end up speaking to no one. You need to be very clear about who you are trying to attract on LinkedIn through social selling.

If you fail to do this, you won't get their attention.

Connect with them emotionally, and you will build a relationship.

If you can speak and connect with a particular community and build a relationship of trust with them, you will have a loyal group of people who WANT what YOU have to offer.

Keep in mind that it is not an industry, business, or organization you are building relationships with, but individuals who are making the decisions. You need to build trust and credibility. And to do that, they need to know three important things about you:

1. You sincerely care

2. You understand their specific problem

3. You have a solution to *their* problem

Your Why Story

The only thing that differentiates you from your competitors is your why!

Watch Simon Sinek's TED Talk, "How great leaders inspire action," and figure out your why. Don't get stuck on what you do or how you do it, but focus rather on the underlying reason why you offer your products or services. Simplify this to a few sentences that reflect your motivations to your ideal clients.

I previously worked with a client who couldn't identify his why. His name is Neal, a financial advisor whose ideal clients were mostly high net worth individuals. I asked him several times why he does what he does, but he couldn't tell me his why. Not until he shared his story from his childhood.

When he was a child, his father lost his business and their family home. Their family of four became very poor and had to move into a one-bedroom apartment. Neal vowed never to let it happen again. And he didn't want the same to happen to anyone else either. That had inspired him to help others grow their wealth, for the safety and security it provided.

In the financial services industry trust is paramount when deciding with whom you want to invest your money. After Neal galvanized his why, he was able to differentiate himself from other financial advisors. He was able to gain substantial trust with new prospects much more quickly.

His business thrived.

How about you? What is your why story?

Write your why story including the related emotional motivations. Keep this brief. Ideally, something that could be shared in a minute or less.

> **EXERCISE**
> What is your why? And how did it come to be?

Your LinkedIn Social Selling Goals

Before you begin your lead generation journey, you also need to determine what your LinkedIn social selling goals are. These goals are your guides at every step while building your strategy and action plan. If you're not sure where to start, begin by reviewing your business goals.

If you have a business plan, identify the goals that can be achieved using lead generation on LinkedIn.

If you don't have a business plan, think of your overall goals for your business. Some examples include:

- Increase brand awareness
- Establish your authority on your topic
- Build a loyal community
- Attract more leads and prospects
- Build relationships with new customers
- Maintain and improve relationships with existing customers
- Improve customer service and retention
- Increase sales and revenue

Determine Your LinkedIn Social Selling Goals

What social selling goals do you want to achieve for your business?

Write down five goals that you want to achieve using LinkedIn. Be as specific as you can, as this will help you determine the KPIs needed to track and measure your success in reaching these goals.

> **EXERCISE**
> List the goals you want to achieve with LinkedIn and social selling. What KPIs will you use to measure the success of these goals?

Takeaways

"It's not what you know but who you know."

This saying only emphasizes that the key to having a successful business is developing relationships.

And to make sure this is happening, there are three critical methods:

1. Take the time to know who they are

2. Listen to the language they use

3. Understand the challenges they face

These methods work most effectively if you have defined who your ideal clients are, if you know your why, and if you have clear goals. This is the foundation for building a compelling LinkedIn profile and social selling strategy.

**Download your FREE companion workbook
that includes all of these exercises and more at
http://LinkedInUnlockedWorkbook.com**

CHAPTER THREE

TRANSFORM YOUR LINKEDIN PROFILE TO ATTRACT CLIENTS

Having a compelling and professional profile is critical to your success on LinkedIn and social selling. This is a pre-requisite before you actively use LinkedIn as a lead generation or business building tool. 50 percent of buyers avoid sales professionals with incomplete LinkedIn profiles.[7]

"Melonie, I have never forgotten what you told me the first time I met you," Greg said.

Greg is a sales expert and highly-rated speaker. He went on to say, *"You said your LinkedIn profile is more important than your website."*

Don't get me wrong; your website is essential. I, myself, invest heavily in my website and the ongoing content I publish on my blog. Still, I believe that your LinkedIn profile often has greater weight than your website.

The first thing that someone does when they want to learn more about you is Google your name. Your LinkedIn profile shows up at the top of the search results and is often the first thing they'll click on to learn more about you. Of all the social media platforms, it's where they can learn the most about you professionally.

That means your LinkedIn profile is often your very **first** online impression.

What kind of impression does your profile currently make?

This is what this chapter is all about. To help you have a profile that you can be proud of, one that represents you the way you want to be seen, and, more importantly, one that is designed to attract clients.

A professional and compelling LinkedIn profile is vital because it:

- Attracts leads and clients organically
- Enhances your professional reputation
- Builds your credibility and authority
- Establishes trust much faster
- Facilitates relationships with decision makers
- Stands out and leaves a lasting impression

We will optimize your LinkedIn profile to make it look professional and client-focused, one that will represent your personal brand well.

People Connect with People

No matter to whom you are selling, whether it's a small business or a large company, the decision is made by a person. People connect with people, not brands.

Businesses often ask me how they can get more traction with their LinkedIn Company Page. My answer is don't focus on your Company Page (some exceptions apply). The magic happens through a personal profile. Your results will come from building relationships with people.

Figure 3.01

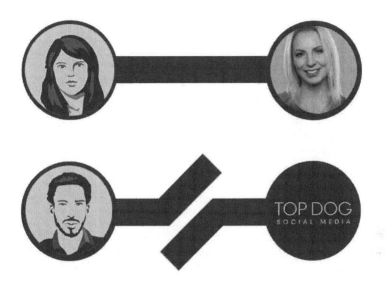

Seven Seconds to Impress

Seven seconds—that's all it takes, and that's all you have to wow a potential client, whether in person or in the digital realm. A well-written and client-focused LinkedIn profile makes the difference in gaining a connection or being ignored. To attract a decision-maker, put your best foot forward.

Your social selling success or lack thereof depends heavily on how your LinkedIn profile represents you and your brand. I've made this easy for you by teaching you the seven steps to optimize your profile and attract clients.

Seven Steps to Attract Your Ideal Client

Step 1. Get Found

Wouldn't it be nice if you showed up in the search results when a prospect was looking for someone like you and what you offer? Your results with social selling are probably not going to come from passively waiting around for someone to find you, but sometimes that can happen. The key is to use the right keywords to make sure that you can be easily found on LinkedIn by anyone who may be looking for the product/service you offer.

Step 2. Your Why Story

Getting found isn't enough. Without giving your ideal clients a compelling reason to pay attention to you or what you have to say, you can guarantee that they'll skip over your profile and move on to the next person. The only thing that truly differentiates you from your competitors is your why story.

Step 3. Credibility

Any relationship between you and your target audience must be built upon a strong foundation of trust. As your profile is the first thing they'll get to see about you, it has to be clear in demonstrating that you are, indeed, credible and worthy of their trust and confidence.

Question: What would make you appear credible in their eyes?

Answer: Recommendations from people who have credibility in the eyes of your prospects.

The more recommendations you have and the more detailed each one is, the higher your ability will be to establish trust with those who read your profile. A recommendation on LinkedIn is different from testimonials on a website (that are often fake); it has a direct link to the person who recommended you, making it much more legitimate.

Additionally, while Skill Endorsements do not hold the same weight as Recommendations, there is still an element of social proof to be found in skills that have frequently been endorsed.

Your achievements and your experience also help further establish your credibility. Honors, awards, and any form of recognition or accolades will raise your reputation as far as your target audience is concerned. This is where you will include some of your bragging rights, whether that would be published works or any other accomplishments. Lastly, share high profile clients you've worked with and any other form of social proof to give you extra credibility.

Step 4. Ideal Clients

If an ideal client were to read your profile, would they quickly realize that you could be the solution they are looking for to solve a problem they are currently facing? Your profile must speak to your ideal clients and, more specifically, the problems they face. Make sure your summary and experience sections highlight precisely who your ideal clients are and how you can help them.

Step 5. CTA (Call-to-Action)

A CTA (or call-to-action) answers one question: What do you want the reader to do next?

Without this one small detail, most people will leave your profile not taking action.

CTAs can come in different forms and with different purposes. You can create a CTA to invite your readers to download a free resource, schedule a consultation, email or call you, and so on. Add a CTA to your LinkedIn profile to help you get leads and facilitate further engagement between you and your potential clients. Make it easy for potential prospects to know what to do next by telling them exactly what you want them to do with your CTA.

Step 6. Authority

You must demonstrate in your profile that you possess the authority and knowledge to solve the problems your ideal clients have. Include within your profile some additional resources that help position your authority, such as LinkedIn Publisher posts and a video of you speaking or teaching on your topic.

Step 7. Stand Out

Ultimately, effective LinkedIn profile optimization involves making sure that you will be noticed in the vast ocean of players in your industry. Grab your rightful piece of the pie with a professional and compelling LinkedIn profile that:

- Includes a professional headshot as your profile photo
- Showcases a headline that captures the attention of your ideal clients
- Incorporates rich media (videos, SlideShare presentations, or PDFs)
- Displays a professional cover photo
- Features recommendations and endorsements for social proof

I was speaking at an event in San Diego, and Stephanie approached me after my talk. Stephanie shared with me that she had followed these exact steps that she had previously learned from me. Shortly after making these changes to her LinkedIn profile, an event planner contacted her on LinkedIn, and she was asked to speak at a conference with more than 8,000 attendees.

Your Personal Brand

Whether you like it or not, in this digital age, everyone has a personal brand. **Personal branding** is defined as the practice of people marketing themselves and their careers as brands. Personal branding is essentially the ongoing process of establishing a prescribed image or impression in the mind of others about an individual, group, or organization.

Your personal brand already exists. The question is: Does it reflect how you want to be seen and known?

Building a strong and professional personal brand is not an option; it is a requirement.

It is key to making connections with your ideal clients and building a relationship on social media—it is especially important on LinkedIn. This is because your personal profile, not a Company Page, does all the heavy lifting on LinkedIn.

This works in your favor, as people always buy from other people. While it may be a company that ultimately purchases your goods or services, it is a person with whom you must first connect and build a relationship to move towards getting the sale.

With this in mind, there are three things your personal brand (and LinkedIn profile) must do:

1. Build Authority and Credibility

Your LinkedIn personal profile must effectively build credibility and position your authority on your topic. Viewers need to know that you are credible.

2. Describe How You Solve Your Prospects' Problems

Demonstrate how you solve the problem your prospects have. No one cares about your business; they only care about their own biggest problem. Be the solution they are looking for. Make sure that is described in your profile.

3. Increase Trust and Engagement

The ultimate goal of your LinkedIn profile (personal brand) is to develop and increase trust and inspire prospects to connect and engage with you.

Keyword Optimization

There will be times when someone is searching for a person who has the solution that you offer. If potential clients are looking on LinkedIn for the products or services you provide and you're not showing up in their search, that's a lost opportunity. You want to keyword optimize your profile so you will show up in the search results;this is what is meant by *optimizing your profile.*

You are already familiar with how people search on Google. How they search on LinkedIn, however, is very different from how they search on Google. On Google, they are searching for information, whereas on LinkedIn they are searching for a person.

For example, if someone is looking on Google for information on how to create an excellent LinkedIn, the person might search using the keyword phrase, *how to create a LinkedIn profile.*

On LinkedIn, they'll search for a person to teach them how to create an excellent LinkedIn profile or even write their LinkedIn profile for them. In this case, the person might search using keywords such as *LinkedIn expert, LinkedIn consultant*, or *LinkedIn profile writer.*

People will often look for title-based keywords on LinkedIn.

LINKEDIN PRO TIP

Before you begin making changes to your LinkedIn profile, especially if you're doing a complete revamp, it is **a good idea to** turn off your Notifications.

You do this by going to the Settings & Privacy page and selecting Privacy. Under Profile privacy click on Sharing profile edits. If this setting is set to Yes, click on it to set it to No. It will auto-save.

Figure 3.02

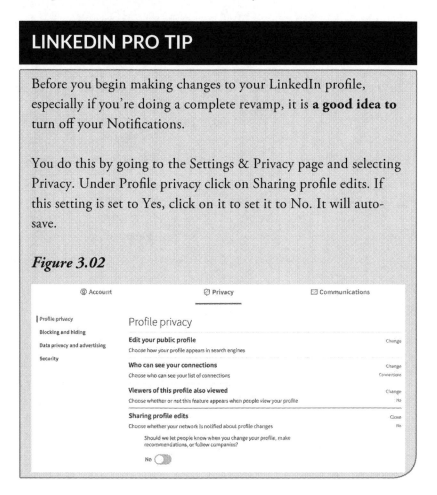

Sections in Your LinkedIn Profile

Your Profile Headline

Your next step is to create a compelling LinkedIn headline. Your headline is the MOST critical part of your profile because, along with your name and profile photo, it is the first thing anyone will see.

Your headline is a great place to include at least one or two keywords. This is important to help you be found by LinkedIn's algorithm so you will show up in the search results.

Of course, it is not enough to merely show up in the search results, because many other profiles will as well. To stand out, you should also ensure that your headline captures your readers' attention and intrigues them enough to want to click on your profile.

Your headline may include any of the following:

- Highlights of your credibility
- Insights into what you do and for whom
- Outcomes/solutions you offer clients

You **only have 120 characters**, and I suggest you use them all to inspire people to click on your profile to learn more about you.

Contact Information

Next, you need to update your contact information. You can include your email, your phone number, and any other information you want people to see. You can also opt out of sharing your personal information such as phone number.

Vanity URL

By default, LinkedIn will automatically create a URL for you. The URL will include your first name, dot, last name, forward slash, a series of numbers with a dash, and another string of numbers.

A vanity URL lets you change the unique link from random, hard to remember letters and numbers to something simple and memorable, like your name.

You should change the URL you are given to a vanity URL. If at all possible, you should select your name for your vanity URL. If your name is not available, try adding a middle initial or a designation at the end.

LINKEDIN PRO TIP

I caution you not to use your company name here because this is your personal profile. There is no guarantee that you will own or work for the same business in the future, but your name will still be your name. Secure your personal name.

For example, my vanity URL is: **LinkedIn.com/in/ MelonieDodaro**

Your Website(s)

In your contact information, you can include your website. Customize the website label instead of it showing only as "Company Website."

LinkedIn gives you three spots to include websites, so if you have more than one website, include up to three of them in this section. If you only have one website, you can still take advantage of all three. For example, you may set one to go to your homepage, another to a service page, or perhaps to a landing page for a download you are offering. This will encourage people to visit the specific pages where you can provide more information about your business offerings.

Figure 3.03

Contact Info

Your Profile

linkedin.com/in/meloniedodaro

Websites

TopDogSocialMedia.com (Digital Sales & Marketing)

LinkedInUnlockedBook.com (LinkedIn Unlocked Book/Bonuses)

LiCodeWebinar.com (FREE LinkedIn Training)

Client-Focused Summary Section

Once somebody lands on your profile, your summary section becomes tremendously crucial because it's where they can learn more about you, versus just about your employment history. Here are some ways to create an effective summary section that speaks to your ideal client:

- Your LinkedIn profile should not be a resume/CV (unless you are looking for a job) or a bio that's written with you as the only focus. This is where you can share your why story.

- Write the summary in the first person. Even though it is business-oriented, LinkedIn is still a social network, so don't forget to be social. One way to do this is to write in the first person, not in the third person.

- Speak directly to your target market. When they land on your profile, you want your potential clients to know they're in the right place and that you are the right person to help them with their specific problem. This is also a place where you'll want to include some keywords that you want to optimize your profile for.

Your summary can be **up to 2,000 characters**; use as many as possible. The most effective formula for writing a compelling and client-focused summary section includes making sure that you address your:

1. Credibility

2. Ideal clients—their problem—your solution

3. Call-to-action

First, start with your **credibility section**. This should contain one or two paragraphs that will tell prospective clients a little bit about who you are, your story, why you do what you do, and your background. Mention accomplishments that will enhance your credibility such as media attention, publications, well-known clients, years of experience, or anything else that makes you stand out. This establishes your credibility in what you do.

The beginning of your summary section is critical as it is visible just below your headline and photo. To see your full summary, someone would have to click the Show more link, which will open the rest of the summary section. You need to be able to capture the viewers' interest so that they want to click to see (and learn) more.

Next, identify your **ideal clients**. This will allow prospective clients to recognize themselves and to know they are in the right place. This is where everything we covered in Chapter 2 becomes vital. You identify the types of clients you work with and then speak directly to them about **their problems** and **your solutions** to those problems.

Mostly, you want to ensure that once your ideal clients land on your profile, they will self-select themselves after realizing that you are someone they need to connect with.

Finally, you should have a clear call-to-action—tell prospective clients exactly what you want them to do next. Do you want them to pick up the phone and call you? Do you want them to email you? Tell them what they should do next with clear and concise directions.

Let me share what I included in my Summary Section as an example of how I put the three-part formula into practice. In my **credibility** section, I tell viewers:

- A little about myself and my story

- How others consider me an authority and have named me on many "top influencer" lists

- About my media coverage

- About my bestselling author status and international keynote speaker at conferences

In my **client-focused** section, I speak directly to my ideal clients. I identify them using the labels I have determined, acknowledge their needs and problems, and then briefly describe my solutions. One of the services I offer is Social Selling Training for sales teams, and my target audience for that is VPs of Sales; they will see right away that I am speaking to them— I've identified them, the problem they face, and my solution to increase the performance of their sales team with social selling training.

I close with my call-to-action, telling them what I want them to do:

Want to know how to turn cold connections into clients on LinkedIn and have a full sales pipeline? Email info@TopDogSocialMedia.com

If you miss this part, you are leaving it to chance that they will take action. People often have the best of intentions and plan to follow up, yet usually don't.

Tell them exactly what to do and tell them to take that action now.

Current Work Experience

This section describes what you're doing right now in your business or your current position. It is also another opportunity to optimize your profile with keywords in your title and your description. Just like the Summary section, you have **2,000 characters to describe your current work experience**, so make sure you make full use of them.

If you have more than one business or more than one focus within your business, you can create two or more current work experience sections. This is what I have done in my profile. I have one current experience section that talks about my digital sales and marketing agency, Top Dog Social Media, what we do and who we are. The second section I have focuses on the speaking aspect of my business and lists the keynote presentations I offer on social selling and LinkedIn.

The formula you use for your current work experience is similar to how you laid out your summary, but with some minor differences.

First, begin with your company credibility section. This is where you talk about the company you work for or the company you own. Share the most compelling information about your company here.

I worked with a company that has been operating for more than 100 years, and nowhere in the company profile or on any of the employee profiles does it say that. I stumbled upon this information on the company's website. This is compelling and showcases their credibility. Many Fortune 500 companies have not been around for 20 years, never mind 100 years. That's a powerful piece of information that will increase a company's credibility and inspire trust. It should absolutely be included in the description.

Next you can list the services you offer and the benefits you provide.

There are a couple of optional things you might consider adding to your current work experience. The first one is a list of current and past clients. Especially if you have well-known clients or brands you've worked with, include their names for social proof. If they're not well-known brands, you can just list the types of clients you work with. For example, you might say, *"We work with accounting and law firms, financial services companies, etc."*

Another possibility is to add one powerful client testimonial. If you have a great client testimonial on your website that isn't shown as a recommendation on your LinkedIn profile, you can include it here.

Lastly, in the description of your current work experience, include a call-to-action. You can use the same call-to-action that you created in the summary section, or a variation of it, and add it to the bottom of your description section.

Rich Media

LinkedIn has a rich media feature that allows you to add videos, SlideShare presentations, and PDFs. Adding multimedia to your summary and current work experience sections makes your profile look more visually appealing and provides viewers more information about you.

Adding video to your profile is very effective in humanizing you and connecting with your viewers. You may also include a product video, a company video, or a testimonial video. PDFs can be white papers or marketing materials describing your products or services. You can also include SlideShare presentations with content you want to share. If you do add multimedia, be sure the content is both relevant and professional in appearance.

Figure 3.04

You can add multimedia while you are editing your profile. At the bottom of the Edit box, you can hit the Upload button to add a presentation, document, or image. In the case of uploaded files, file size may not exceed 300 MB.

Click the Link button to link to videos, photos, documents, or SlideShare presentations that exist online that you want to include.

Hit Save at the bottom of the box once you have finished adding your rich media.

Figure 3.05

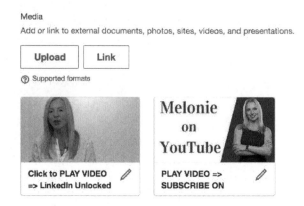

Past Experience

Your past experience doesn't need to be as comprehensive as your current experience, but should at least include a paragraph describing relevant past experience so that your profile looks complete.

You don't need to list every job you've had since high school, but make sure this section is complete and includes at least some of your past work experience.

Skills

Take advantage of the skills section of your profile, and include a list of the skills you possess. This is also a great place to add the keywords you want to be found for. The skills you list can then be endorsed by your connections. Be sure that the three most relevant skills you want to be recognized for are listed at the top.

Figure 3.06

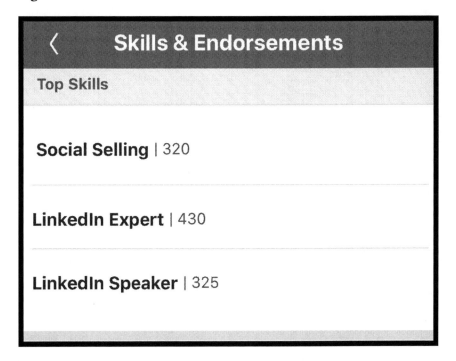

Volunteer Experience

Your volunteer experience should go in this section. Make sure that you add all of your volunteer experience in this section.

The volunteer experience section isn't a default section within your profile—add it by clicking on the Add profile section button below your headline on your profile. Click on the "+" icon to add Volunteer experience under the Background section.

Education

Now you need to complete your Education section. This is very basic and easy to do. Insert your post-secondary education in this section.

Accomplishments

There are many other vital areas in your LinkedIn profile that you should update to ensure that your profile:

- Looks professional and complete

- Further establishes your credibility and authority

- Helps your ideal clients to know, like, and trust you

If you want to add the different Accomplishment sections to your profile, you'll need to manually add these, just as you did with your volunteer experience.

There are many different categories under Accomplishments, which include:

- **Publications**: List your published work and be found seven times more

- **Certifications**: List a certification and get five times more profile views

- **Courses**: List coursework from your prior or continuing education

- **Projects**: Add compelling projects to demonstrate your experience

- **Honors & Awards**: Include any awards, accolades, or recognition you've received

- **Patents**: Showcase your innovation and expertise

- **Test Scores**: List a test score here if you excelled in an exam (this is especially good for recent graduates)

- **Languages**: Show how you can be a fit for a job or overseas opportunity

- **Organizations**: Show your involvement with communities that are important to you

While these sections are available for you to fill out, you only want to include them if they are relevant to you. Many of these sections can be particularly beneficial to add for credibility and authority building, if they are relevant.

Publications is an excellent section to help you establish your authority on your topic. Include content or resources you have created that are of value to your ideal clients and showcase your expertise. These could include books, eBooks, reports, whitepapers, or articles you have written.

Add any honors and awards you and your business have received, as this is an excellent way to establish your authority and credibility. You can also list any media attention you've received.

There is also an additional section where you can add your certifications that are not appropriate to add in the Education section.

Recommendations

Finally, I strongly advise that you get recommendations on your profile, as this provides essential social proof. When people are deciding with whom to do business, they are often swayed by the decisions others have made, so the more recommendations you have, the better. Quality recommendations are important. Ask for at least five to ten recommendations from credible people who can genuinely vouch for who you are and what you do.

LINKEDIN PRO TIP

When asking someone for a LinkedIn recommendation, do NOT use the default message. Instead, customize both the subject line and the message.

When you ask people for a recommendation, there can be a few things that may prevent them from doing so—even for those who know and respect you and want to give you one.

For example, if your recommendation request comes when they're busy, they may think to themselves, *"Oh, I'll get back to that when I have time."* Or, *"I don't know what to write right now, so I'll take care of this later."* And they never do, because they continue to put it off or forget.

Others might find the task difficult because they are unsure of what to write. Again, they likely will never get around to it.

How to Get LinkedIn Recommendations

The key to getting recommendations is to strike when the iron is hot.

Each time I receive some form of testimonial or praise via email or private message, I thank them and then ask if they would be comfortable writing that on a LinkedIn recommendation.

For example, after reading my last book someone sent me a private message on LinkedIn and said, *"Melonie, I just wanted to tell you that after I finished reading your book last week, I implemented what I learned, and that resulted in a $4,000 sale."*

First, I congratulated the person. After all, I love implementers. Implementers always get results. Then I said, *"Thank you for sharing that with me; that would make a fantastic LinkedIn recommendation. Are you open to writing that in a recommendation for me?"*

You should also reach out to people with whom you have worked in the past and request a recommendation. It's important to let people know why you are asking for one. You must customize your message, and it could be as simple as this:

"I recently read a book on LinkedIn and have been working on improving my profile. The next step is to get some recommendations. Would you be willing to write one for me about the project we worked on together? I'd really appreciate it."

Having a complete and professional profile with recommendations provides social proof that will significantly improve your social selling efforts.

Before you read any further, please go ahead and complete all of the different sections of your profile that I've described in this chapter.

When you do this, you will have a compelling and professional LinkedIn profile that will ensure you are ready to start connecting with prospects and generating new business on LinkedIn.

CHAPTER FOUR

LINKEDIN BEST PRACTICES AND ETIQUETTE

When using LinkedIn, there are spoken and unspoken rules.

In this chapter, I am going to cover the best business practices to follow when using LinkedIn to generate leads through social selling. If you don't follow proper etiquette, you risk damaging your credibility, and your social selling results will be dismal.

If wasting your time and hurting your credibility isn't enough reason to pay close attention to these best practices, perhaps having your account restricted or entirely removed by LinkedIn will. This can happen if you don't adhere to these fundamental principles for using LinkedIn effectively.

I will share with you the mistakes you must avoid, the types of posts that can damage your personal brand, and the skills necessary to succeed with LinkedIn and social selling.

Social Selling Best Practices and LinkedIn Etiquette

Personalize

The first and most important best practice I can share with you is to personalize every connection request that you send out to people you don't know at all or don't know well.

I get it. LinkedIn makes it VERY easy to accidentally send the default connection request on desktop and, especially, on the mobile app. You must consciously and actively avoid sending the default invitation; take the time to do a little research and write a personalized connection request.

This one best practice will be the difference between someone clicking Accept or Ignore in response to your connection request. If someone clicks Ignore, they will also have the option to select "I don't know this person."

WARNING: If you receive an excessive number of "I don't know this person" responses, your account could be restricted, and this will destroy your ability to connect with prospects and expand your network.

Personalizing your invites is **not** optional if you want to succeed at social selling and to connect with new prospects. If you follow just this one tip, you will significantly increase your success on LinkedIn, as most people are not doing it, and your invite will stand out. I receive hundreds of connection requests every month, and still, fewer than five percent of them are personalized in any way. In fact, personalized invites are so rare that when I see one, I almost always accept it.

Later in this book, I'll go into detail and provide you with examples of connection request messages you could use when connecting with someone new on LinkedIn.

Send a Welcome Message

You've connected with someone on LinkedIn. Now what?

Think about this. Would you complain about not getting any new leads from attending a networking function if all you did was collect business cards and never follow up with anyone? How do you expect a LinkedIn connection to turn into anything other than a random connection if you never make contact beyond the initial connection request?

I've spoken at so many events where people have said, *"I don't ever get leads from LinkedIn."* Out of all these people, the majority never progressed beyond sending and receiving connection requests. You can't magically expect business to appear just by being on LinkedIn or any other social network for that matter.

As I stated in the introduction of this book, I believe when you stop collecting connections and start building relationships, you increase trust and credibility; you attract more clients. Stop collecting connections; it's time to build relationships if you want to succeed with LinkedIn.

How do you do that?

You start by sending a short, yet friendly welcome message after your connection request is accepted. In this message, you want to thank them for connecting and show some interest in them.

For example, you may compliment them on something within their profile, their business, or something they have recently shared on LinkedIn. If you can find any commonality with them, such as shared experience interests or connections, bring that up. This is the start of your relationship-building process on LinkedIn. And whatever you do, do NOT ask them for anything in this message. If you do, the possibility of a relationship will be over.

To get to know your connection, it is crucial to follow this step. It is the difference between merely adding contacts to your network and building real relationships. No matter how many connections you have, they will be of no benefit if you do not take the time and effort to build relationships with your connections.

Irrelevant Messages are Spam

The term spam means different things to different people. To me, spam is anything that the receiver doesn't find value in. Make sure that any message you send to a connection is entirely relevant to them, otherwise don't be surprised when they don't respond or mark it as spam.

For example, I often get messages from people who ask if I am interested in learning how to use LinkedIn for business and inviting me to their "LinkedIn Basics" webinar. They have not taken the time to read my profile or learn that I have written and created multiple online courses and books about LinkedIn and that I speak and train globally on the topic.

Also, I regularly get messages from people inviting me to attend their lunch-time networking event in a city 5,000 miles away.

Some people use automation tools that send mass messages to all of their connections. These can be dangerous on LinkedIn for this exact reason. With the use of these automation tools, people send their entire LinkedIn network a message that is irrelevant to 90 percent or more of their entire network. Nothing can diminish the possibility of a relationship with a potential prospect faster than receiving inappropriate messages from you.

Do NOT send your connections anything sales related or irrelevant; they will consider that spam. Everything you send to your connections should be positioned for their benefit, not yours, if you want to stand a chance at building a relationship with them.

Respond to Messages/Reply Promptly

Similar to an email, the promptness of your response is often just as important as the message itself.

If you are sending messages to your new connections, some of them are very likely to reply. Check your LinkedIn inbox regularly, and respond to the messages you receive.

This is exactly what people think when they receive a message from you—that you are open for some form of conversation—so responding to them when they reply to you is critical. And this is also why, in all of the best practices I've covered before, this one is so important.

Who's Viewed Your Profile

Are you looking at who's viewed your LinkedIn profile? If you are not, you could be missing out on possible prospects who have already shown an interest in you.

People are searching for people on LinkedIn, and if they've come across your profile and not taken the initiative to send you a connection request, this is your chance to reach out to them.

If there is someone who's viewed your profile with whom you would like to be a connection, reach out with a personalized connection request just the way you would to any other potential prospect. There's no need to include, *"I saw you viewed my profile,"* in your message.

You can also get some additional insights in the Who's Viewed Your Profile section including what companies your viewers work at, the job title(s) of those who are viewing your profile most often, and how they are finding you.

If you have a free LinkedIn membership, you will see only the last five people who have viewed your account. However, paid memberships enable you to see everyone who has viewed your profile in the previous 90 days.

Professional Headshot

People are visual, and the first thing we notice in a LinkedIn profile is the profile picture photo. According to LinkedIn, profiles with headshots are 14 times more likely to be viewed than those without a profile picture.

You must have a photo of you. Not a company logo. Not a family vacation picture. A professional headshot of you. Don't miss the opportunity to make a great first impression by ensuring that the image is set with a clean background and focuses on your eyes and smile.

Remember: this is your personal brand, and you only have seconds to make a positive impression.

Your Profile Must Pass Their *WIIFM* Filter

One of the biggest mistakes made on LinkedIn is writing a profile all about you and not speaking to your ideal clients. The truth is nobody cares about you; they don't care about your business or what you sell—they only care about what you can do for them.

People are always viewing your profile through their *WIIFM* filter— *what's in it for me?*

Speak directly to your target market. When someone lands on your profile, you want your potential clients to know they're in the right place and that you are the person who can help them with their specific problems.

The exercises completed in Chapters 2 and 3 (creating a client-focused profile), ensure you are passing your prospects' *WIIFM* filter.

Name Field

Adding something other than your name in the name field is a violation of LinkedIn's Terms of Service and can get your account restricted. But beyond this breach of contract, using something other than your name makes you harder to find, looks unprofessional, and reduces your credibility.

There are exceptions. These include things such as suffixes, e.g. Ph.D., as well as former names, maiden names, and nicknames (as these can make it easier to find you by those who know you).

LinkedIn's Terms of Service state that it is unacceptable to add personal information such as email addresses or phone numbers, or to use symbols, numbers, or special characters.

Bye Bye Boring Headline and Summary

When someone lands on your LinkedIn profile, you have seconds to impress them and make them want to learn more about you. The very first thing they will see is your headline and the beginning of your Summary section. If you don't grab their attention, they will click away, and the opportunity is lost.

You have 120 characters in your headline to tell people who you are and what you do. You can further expand on this in the first couple lines of your Summary section. This is where you can inspire your viewer to click Show more, to open up your complete Summary section and learn more about you.

Your Activity

It is extremely easy for anyone viewing your profile to see just how active… or rather inactive you are on LinkedIn.

Your activity and engagement will keep you top of mind with your connections and are crucial ingredients to relationship-building. You cannot build relationships if you aren't present and engaging in conversations with your prospects.

A great way to stay active and visible is by posting a status update regularly, as well as posting to LinkedIn Publisher if you write articles. It's also very essential to engage with the posts and articles of your connections in your newsfeed by liking, commenting, and sharing when relevant.

Privacy Settings

Privacy settings are there for your protection, but don't forget this is a professional platform where you want to grow your network. LinkedIn is the place where you share your professional background and not all of your personal information and family photos, so you can be much more open when deciding with whom to connect.

With this in mind, allow your profile to be public, make sure your full name is visible to all of your connections, that people are notified when you are in the news, and that your connections can see your connection list.

If there are some people with whom you don't want to share your information, then they shouldn't be a part of your network, and you should remove them as a connection.

LINKEDIN PRO TIP

One important setting you should change is the one that says, Viewers of this profile also viewed. This is located on the Settings & Privacy page.

This is the LinkedIn default, and it will often display your competitors along the side of your profile—turn this **off** as you don't want to send people to visit your competitors' profiles.

Never Add Connections to Your Email List

Do not export your connection list and add them to your email database or send them messages through a third-party email marketing service provider. Just because someone has connected with you on LinkedIn does NOT give you permission to add them to your list and send them emails. Not to mention it is illegal in some countries.

Regardless of what country you are in, you are still liable when sending emails to people where these regulations apply, such as Canada with their CAN-SPAM Act and European Union with their GDPR privacy law. There are strict penalties for violations.

Whether this is illegal or not in the country where you are located, it is a highly unethical marketing practice that should be avoided entirely.

Social Proof

Social proof shows that others have trusted you to engage in your services, have been happy working with you, and received the results they were looking for. It is vital that you include social proof in your LinkedIn profile.

Social proof dramatically increases your credibility and ability to establish yourself as an authority. LinkedIn has made social proof easy by incorporating sections for Recommendations and Skills & Endorsements on your profile.

Recommendation Requests

Always personalize your requests for recommendations. There are default messages for many LinkedIn functions, including this one, but I never recommend you use them. Always customize messages, including recommendation requests.

Nurture Relationships

Nurture your LinkedIn relationships through regular engagement. LinkedIn will notify you with trigger events such as when one of your connections starts a new job or is mentioned in the news. Take a moment to congratulate them with a personalized message.

If you come across an article or resource or something in the news that would be relevant to someone in your network, reach out to them personally with a note and share it with them.

When someone is commenting on your content, reply back to them. If someone shares your content, comment on it and thank them for sharing it.

Use LinkedIn's notifications, and pay attention to the newsfeed to find trigger events that make it easy to reach out to someone and nurture the relationship.

Use LinkedIn and social selling "the go-giver way," made popular by the author, Bob Burg. **Create value, touch lives, build networks, be real, and stay open.**

Post Valuable Content

Sharing content is essential to stay top of mind with your network. But only if it's the right content and is considered valuable in the minds of your ideal prospects and clients. When sharing content, whether it's your own or it's curated content, your goal must always be to provide value to your target audience.

Introduce People

This is a LinkedIn best practice that can create significant social capital for you: introduce your connections to each other when it makes sense. Think of yourself as a business matchmaker. Doing this will invoke reciprocity[8], and often people will return the favor and introduce you to some of their connections, thus expanding your network in a very personal way. This is an excellent opportunity to support your connections and continue to nurture relationships.

The people you have introduced will likely think of you when they come across someone who needs what you offer and often will reciprocate with an introduction.

Keep It Positive and Professional

There's a difference between taking a stand or having an opinion, and attacking and criticizing others. There's often a lot of schoolyard-style bullying that happens on social media. Do not participate in this.

Avoid criticizing anyone publicly. I often see people in heated debates, which serve no purpose other than to turn many people off.

Remember: LinkedIn is not Facebook or Twitter. This is a professional network.

Keep things professional, or you risk losing your credibility and trust with your connections. This doesn't mean you can't ever post anything of a personal nature, but limit it, and consider your audience on LinkedIn before doing so.

Keep your comments positive, and avoid wasting your time in point-less debates; after all, you have some new business to generate!

LinkedIn Open Networker (LION)

While becoming a LION (LinkedIn Open Networker) may seem like an excellent way to grow your network quickly, it is neither efficient nor effective. A LION is a person who will accept a connection request from everyone and anyone who sends them one.

Now you might be thinking, *"Don't I want to build an extensive network?"*

Yes, you do. But the quality is much more important than the quantity of your network, and you should be focused on connecting with the right people.

If a LION accepts a connection request from absolutely anyone, you can be sure their network will include spammers and fake accounts. Your network will be far more useful if you focus on connecting with reputable people and targeted prospects.

LinkedIn Groups

One of the fastest ways to expand your network is to join the right LinkedIn groups. What are the right LinkedIn Groups? They're the ones your ideal clients belong to. To find people through the advanced search on LinkedIn, your network consists of your 1st-, 2nd-, and 3rd-degree connections as well as members of groups you are a part of. (More on this in a later chapter.)

Most people make the mistake of selecting groups that are filled with their industry peers and competitors. It's entirely fine to join some of these groups, but don't miss out on joining the groups that are filled with prospects for you to quickly find and connect with.

LinkedIn Posts That Can Hurt Your Personal Brand

As I have mentioned before, and will remind you again throughout the book, LinkedIn is a social platform for businesses and professionals. It is a professional space, much the same as a business office where you have potential prospects or clients meet with you. If something is not appropriate to be shared with prospects or clients face-to-face in your office, chances are, it is also inappropriate to be shared on LinkedIn as well. Avoid the following four types of posts:

1. Controversial Posts

As LinkedIn is a professional network full of clients, potential clients, industry peers, and other people in professional relationships with you, it is a good idea to avoid topics that tend to polarize people, especially controversial ones with a negative connotation. This is not because these topics are not important or relevant, but because this is not the correct platform for those discussions.

Because these topics do polarize people, discussing them can invoke the age-old "you are either with us or against us" mentality. In these scenarios, if you fall on the opposite side of your clients or other professional relationships, this can hurt your ability to build relationships. In most cases, it is better to avoid posting (or even commenting) on these types of posts altogether.

2. Political or Religious Posts

These are two topics that people feel incredibly passionate about. Just like with controversial topics, these types of posts tend to see people join one camp or another. Your connections can take great offense if you believe differently than they do.

This is one of the reasons why Facebook usage has started to decline, according to digital marketing expert Jay Baer. Baer believes users are growing weary of having to defend their opinions to so-called "friends" who may now be part of the "opposition."

3. Sales Pitch Posts

While LinkedIn is the best platform for B2B, it is most effective when you use it as a platform to build relationships, rather than as a place to broadcast your sales material.

While some businesses can make sales directly on the platform, most will not, and the real success comes from building relationships with your ideal clients and moving that conversation offline. It's offline that you get the chance to speak with your prospect, get to know them and the problems they are facing, and, only then, discuss in a sales conversation the solution you offer.

Focus on providing value and being the go-to resource for your ideal clients so that when they need someone who does what you do, you are the first person who comes to mind.

4. Inappropriate Personal Posts

While you should be social, you can be social AND professional at the same time. That means no cat memes, no posts of what you ate for lunch (unless it is relevant to your profession), no drinking/partying pics, and your LinkedIn connections certainly don't need to know anything about your ex.

LinkedIn Posts That Will Enhance Your Personal Brand

Just as some information is inappropriate to be shared on LinkedIn, other types of posts, like the four I explain in detail below, can bolster your authority with your network, create more engagement, keep you top of mind, and enhance your overall personal brand:

1. Timely and Relevant Posts

There is no better way to create a conversation with your connections (helping you to stay top of mind) and increase engagement than to post on timely and relevant topics in the news that are relevant to your network.

In addition to sharing this information, you want to include your insights and perspective as additional commentary to the post. After all, your connections may see the same news shared by many people, but your perspective on it makes your post unique.

2. Conversation Inspiring Posts

While you want to avoid negative, non-business-related topics, it can be good to post on topics that can inspire productive debate on critical issues in your industry or the business world.

Both the content and how you present it should be thoughtful and inspire productive conversation rather than emotionally heated debates.

3. Professional Changes or Wins Posts

A great way to occasionally add a bit of yourself into your LinkedIn status updates is to share relevant professional or work-related wins and changes. This could be a new job, a promotion, getting a new client, or a lesson learned.

This a great way to get people to know you better and learn what you are up to professionally.

4. Personal Touch Posts

You might be thinking, *"But you just said to keep it professional."* And I did.

But occasionally, and done correctly, it can be beneficial to share something more personal with your connections.

It may be related to a cause you believe in, a philanthropic project, a personal lesson you learned, or a story that is relatable to others.

10 Skills You Need to Succeed with Social Selling

While I have shared a lot of what you should or shouldn't do, I also wanted to share with you some of the skills you already possess that you probably learned as early as grade school. Activating these skills will help you to succeed with social selling:

1. Don't Forget Your Manners

Never underestimate the power of proper etiquette—aka common sense and good manners. Remember to say please and thank you. Show gratitude when people engage with you and your posts by acknowledging them.

2. Adjust to New Situations

Speaking to new people can feel risky or uncomfortable—but communication is the key to relationship-building on LinkedIn.

It is essential that you can step out of your comfort zone and send personalized messages and connection requests to potential clients.

3. Attempt New Things Knowing It's Okay to Make Mistakes

Don't be one of those people whose LinkedIn profile sits inactive for years because you are afraid of making a mistake.

Everyone makes mistakes. If you make a mistake, apologize (if appropriate), learn the lesson, and move on.

4. Ask for Help

If you have someone you would like to meet, ask someone in your network if they would be comfortable making an introduction.

5. Respect Others

Some people would (and have) argued that you should be able to post whatever you want on any social media platform. That any topic should be fair game and that anything less is censorship or inhibiting the discussion of relevant issues.

I have to disagree. In my opinion, LinkedIn is not appropriate for every topic of discussion. LinkedIn is a business platform. It is a place of professionals.

Before you post something, consider if it is something that you would want to say right in front of a potential client. Because essentially that is what you are doing. If you do get into a debate on a more sensitive topic, be professional, be polite, and, most importantly, BE RESPECTFUL.

6. Cooperate

Collaboration is a powerful community- and business-building strategy. LinkedIn is an excellent platform to find and build relationships with people who you can benefit from collaborating with.

There are people in your network who offer complementary products or services, and they could become great referral partners to you.

7. Offer to Help

Nothing makes a stronger and more genuine impression on somebody than when you give selflessly, generously, and (most importantly) without the expectation of receiving anything in return. This can be as simple as sharing a great piece of content produced by someone in your network.

8. Ask Questions and Express Curiosity

Be curious. Be interested. Asking questions or commenting on the posts and comments of your connections is vital to starting a conversation. This is where real relationship-building begins.

9. Share Ideas

LinkedIn Publisher is a fantastic way to establish your authority and expand your reach on LinkedIn. The ability to share information in a way that is easily understood or relatable is a crucial step when creating content on LinkedIn Publisher.

When you write, you need to make sure that you write your post from the point of view and at the technical level of your audience (and potential customers).

10. Tell Stories

While it might not be appropriate to share a lot of personal information on LinkedIn, it is an excellent place to share professional or work-related stories and experiences.

Engaging storytelling makes people more interested and emotionally invested in what you are sharing. So, draw your readers in (if and where appropriate) with a funny, poignant, or thoughtful post that humanizes you and makes you more relatable and likable.

This list of LinkedIn best practices will provide you with a solid foundation to initiate and build relationships with prospects, establish your credibility, and increase trust throughout your social selling activities.

FIND LEADS AND PROSPECTS ON LINKEDIN

I have developed a lead generation system that is specific to LinkedIn. I call it The LINK Method™. In this chapter, I'll outline the methodology and then reveal precisely how to implement this method in the following chapter.

Five crucial steps make up this process that can turn LinkedIn into a highly predictable lead generator for you.

The LINK Method™ consists of the highest leveraging activities you can do on LinkedIn to generate new clients, and includes these critical five steps:

1. Find prospects

2. Make first contact

3. Engage in dialogue

4. Build relationship

5. Move conversation offline

Most of the B2B professionals and companies I work with have the same goal: book offline conversations with prospects. It's offline that you convert a prospect to a client. However, there are two big mistakes social sellers make when using LinkedIn:

1. Rushing the process and going right into a sales pitch

2. Never moving the conversation offline, or doing this too slowly

Going too fast or too slow can have a detrimental impact on your sales and revenue goals. Let me cover what each of these five steps involves and the delicate balance necessary to make The LINK Method™ work.

Figure 5.01

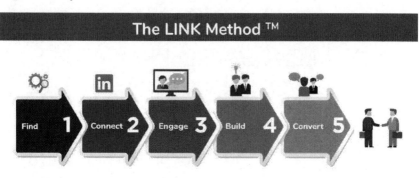

Copyright © TopDogSocialMedia.com

Step 1: Find Prospects

Remember that we talked earlier in the book about creating a clear picture of your perfect client. Understanding and using the language of your ideal client is essential for this step to be successful.

There are two ways to prospect on LinkedIn. The first is by doing a targeted search for prospects, and the second is by leveraging your network to gain introductions.

LINKEDIN PRO TIP

LinkedIn will email you with the number of searches you showed up in each week as well as some of the companies for which the people who were searching work.

Notice any significant changes in numbers from week to week. Compare these changes against your weekly activities. For example, do you appear in more searches on the weeks when you post an article on LinkedIn Publisher or when you comment more often on status updates? Pay attention to trends you notice, and adapt your strategy to take advantage of them.

You can also gain additional insights about the people viewing your profile through the information LinkedIn provides about the job titles people have as well as the companies that they work for. This information may open up a new opportunity to focus on a target market you hadn't previously considered.

Figure 5.02

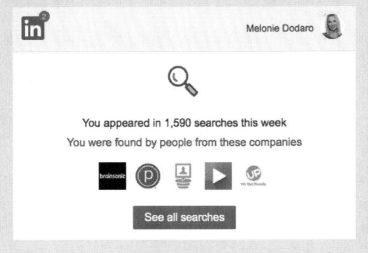

LinkedIn offers you a fantastic ability to find prospects through its Advanced Search function. Depending upon the level of membership you have, the search filters will be different. For example, Sales Navigator offers the most robust set of filters to do highly targeted searches. You can still do searches with a free account or even a Premium account, but you will have fewer search filters available to you in the Advanced Search function.

Using Advanced Search

LinkedIn's Advanced Search tool is excellent for finding potential prospects you can connect with.

The Advanced Search uses what is known as a Boolean search[9], and this gives you the ability to filter your search so that you find exactly what you are looking for. You do this by adding or eliminating elements from the search parameters.

Add Boolean Search Parameters in LinkedIn's Advanced Search

Boolean search allows you to get even more precise when using the Advanced Search tool. For example, you could include and exclude various aspects of your search.

Let's say for example you want to find someone who is an expert in personal branding, and you use that as a keyword in your search. Your search results would pull up someone who has the words "personal" and "branding" in their profile, even if the two words are located separately in their profile. By adding quotes around "personal branding" your search results will only list those profiles with those two words together.

Another example could be, you want to find someone who has expertise in both branding and graphic design; you could do a Boolean search like this: branding AND "graphic design" to get more relevant search results.

Here is a summary of how to use Boolean search in LinkedIn's Advanced Search and all of the different ways you can use it to create a much more targeted search result:

QUOTES

If you would like to search for an exact phrase, you can enclose the phrase in quotation marks. You can use these in addition to other modifiers.

Examples:

"product manager" "account representative" "executive assistant"

PARENTHETICALS

If you would like to do a complex search, you can combine terms and modifiers. For instance, the first example will find both software engineers and software architects.

Examples:

software AND (engineer or architect)

(instructional designer OR instructional design)

e-learning (human resources) AND "customer service"

AND

If you would like to search for profiles that include two terms, you can separate those terms with the upper-case word AND. However, you don't have to use AND—if you enter two terms, the search program will assume that there is an AND between them.

Examples:

software AND engineer

software+engineer [You can also add a plus + in between the words with no space]

"customer service" AND hospitality

"instructional design" AND "e-learning" software engineer

OR

If you would like to broaden your search to find profiles that include one or more terms, you can separate those terms with the uppercase word OR.

Examples:

"Pitney Bowes" OR "Hewlett-Packard"

Helpdesk OR "Help Desk" OR "Technical Support" "Vice President" OR VP OR "V.P." OR SVP OR EVP

"account executive" OR "account exec" OR "account manager" OR "sales executive" OR "sales manager" OR "sales representative"

NOT

If you would like to do a search but exclude a particular term, type that term with an uppercase NOT immediately before it. Your search results will exclude any profile containing that term.

Examples:

NOT director

(Google OR Salesforce) NOT LinkedIn

director NOT executive NOT VP NOT "Vice President"

So, for example, if I were looking for a CEO of a large company, not a small business owner, founder, or consultant, I would use the Boolean tools in the Advanced Search function. In the search box, I could specify the exact search requirements I have. The search may look like this:

CEO NOT Owner NOT Founder NOT Consultant

Figure 5.03

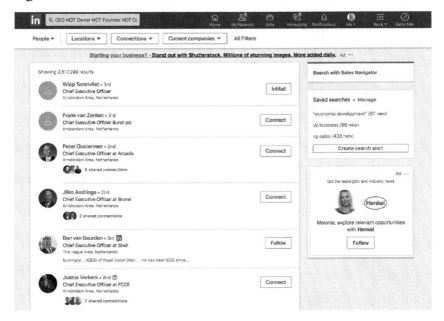

Now, this doesn't mean that all the people who come up will always be perfectly targeted, but it will narrow your search and provide more targeted results. You can continue narrowing your search down by location, by a company, and by other filters to find precisely what you want.

You should also remove 1st-degree connections from your search parameters because they are already part of your network. You are looking for 2nd-degree connections you can connect with. While using a Boolean search will lower the number of results you get, it will also provide more specific and targeted results.

LINKEDIN PRO TIP

If you have a Sales Navigator membership, you can also look at numerous other filters including group members, company size, seniority level, and title. You can also search for Fortune 500, Fortune 100, or Fortune 50 companies.

The extra Advanced Search filters are one of the main differences between the free and Sales Navigator accounts on LinkedIn, which I will discuss in more detail in a later chapter.

Saved Searches

If you find a particular search that is producing good results, you can save that search. This is a powerful tool because you will get search alerts directly from LinkedIn when people match those criteria. You can come back to these search results at any time and check for new potential prospects. You can then go through each of these new profiles and reach out to connect with any who fit your criteria of a prospect.

This feature is currently available with both free and paid membership levels, but the number of saved searches you are permitted varies depending on which actual membership level you have.

Figure 5.04

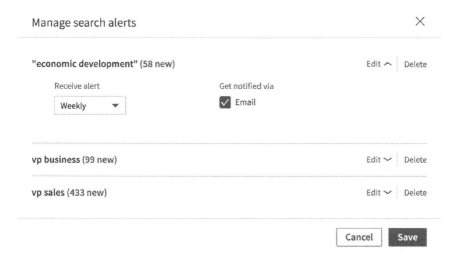

This is LinkedIn sending targeted prospects to your inbox. Furthermore, LinkedIn will send you an email once a week with any new profiles that match your Saved Search parameters. With a free account, you can set up three Saved Search results.

Expand Your LinkedIn Network

As part of your social selling efforts, you need to build a quality network full of your ideal clients, referral partners, and industry peers.

People can only find you if you're in their 1st-, 2nd-, or 3rd-degree networks, or if you're a member of the same group. This makes it important to grow your network. Remember, this isn't Facebook. You don't need to guard and protect your LinkedIn presence or network.

Naturally, you won't connect with anyone who looks suspicious. There could be any number of reasons why you won't want to accept connection requests from certain people, but for the most part, it's good to accept invitations to connect. It's a win-win situation because every single person you connect with expands your network further.

Figure 5.05

One way you can quickly expand your network is to join relevant LinkedIn Groups. LinkedIn allows you to join up to 100 groups, so you can significantly expand the size of your reach (potentially by thousands or even millions of people, many of whom are potential prospects) by joining relevant groups full of your ideal clients.

One big mistake people make is they only join their industry-specific groups. To benefit from the increased network that joining LinkedIn groups provides, you must join groups that **your ideal clients belong to**.

Take a look at some of the groups that your prospects and clients are members of; some of these could be ideal groups for you to join.

If your business focuses on a specific geographic region, then you will want to search out and join all relevant local groups. If, for example, your business focuses on attracting clients in New York, Amsterdam, London,

Hong Kong, or Toronto, just type the specific city name into the search box under Groups, and see which groups come up. Review these groups, and determine which ones might be a good fit for you.

When reviewing groups, there are some specific things you should pay attention to. First, how many members are in the group? The more members a group has, the more your network expands. However, don't discount a group with a smaller number of members if it is a very targeted niche group filled with your ideal clients.

The majority of the groups you join should be groups that your target market belongs to. It is okay for you to consider joining some of your industry-specific groups as well as other groups you have a professional interest in as a way of staying current and knowledgeable.

Growing your network is essential to your prospecting efforts to provide you with search results that generate a significant number of prospects as you are limited to finding people who are within your network.

The other benefit is that you will be found by more people and more often when someone is searching for what you offer.

Step 2: Make First Contact

After you have located potential prospects, you need to make first contact. This process starts with your initial connection request. Make it personalized; give people a reason they should connect with you. What you put in your connection request message will largely determine your success. I'll cover this in detail in the next chapter.

Step 3: Engage in Dialogue

This step consists of establishing rapport and starting a dialogue with your new contact so you can begin to build a relationship with them. You do this by following up with a personalized message. I call this the welcome message. If someone has sent a message to you after accepting your request, keep the conversation going.

Additionally, when a prospect makes first contact with you by sending you a connection request, reply by thanking them for connecting with you. This is also a great chance to start building the relationship by starting a dialogue with them, expressing interest in learning more about them.

Step 4: Build Relationship

The process of building relationships isn't limited to just one message after you connect with a prospect. You'll want to send additional messages to continue the momentum and begin to add some value to them.

LINKEDIN PRO TIP

The content of these messages will depend on your industry and goals, but should NOT include anything that could be perceived as sales materials or a sales pitch of any sort!

Do NOT make the mistake of trying to sell or pitch your product or services in a LinkedIn message. Doing so is the fastest way to kill a potential relationship.

Step 5: Move Conversation Offline

Finally, you need to move the conversation and the relationship to the next level—offline. No relationship with a potential prospect should be kept solely on LinkedIn or on any online platform.

If you have established rapport, built some trust, and provided value to your prospect (essentially earned the right), many of them will be willing to have an offline conversation with you—be it through a phone call, a video call meeting, or even an in-person meeting. It is offline that you get to know your prospect, understand their challenges, and, when appropriate, offer your solution. It's offline that you convert a prospect to a client.

Now that you know the overview of The LINK Method™, and how exactly to find potential prospects on LinkedIn, I will reveal the specific steps and ideal timing of each one, showing you how to go from finding a prospect to moving the conversation offline.

CHAPTER SIX

CONVERT PROSPECTS TO CLIENTS WITH THE LINK METHOD™

I can't tell you how many social selling experts I've heard say that the key to success is through sharing content on LinkedIn.

I disagree!

Content has its role, and it's an important one that I discuss in depth in the next chapter, but content alone is not going to generate a steady stream of new clients. What will is a direct outreach to targeted prospects, which is the fastest, most reliable, and effective way to generate leads and clients on LinkedIn.

Many of my clients and the students I've taught through my workshops and online training programs expressed a similar challenge before working with me. They didn't know what to do after the initial connection request. They had a lot of questions, such as:

- So, we've connected; now what?

- What do I say in a message?

- How do I send a message without coming across as spammy?

- What are the steps I need to follow and in what time frame?

This is precisely why I created The LINK Method™ and broke it down into a simple system to show you exactly what to do, what to say, and when to do it. The LINK Method™ is a system of sending a sequence of messages to a prospect that starts with connecting with them on LinkedIn and moves to an offline conversation.

The success of this comes from the personalization you put into it. But writing brand new messages every time you connect with someone new can be very time-consuming. To create a more efficient process I'll show you how to develop a set of message templates you can use over and over again, just spending a minute or two on adding a level of personalization that captures their attention, so your message doesn't come across as a canned response.

Throughout this chapter, I will share the importance of personalization. I will provide examples of the different messages you should send and create, discuss how you can use trigger events to continue to engage with your prospects, and outline techniques to build and strengthen relationships, enhancing your social selling efforts.

The Importance of Personalization

Earlier I mentioned, even though you may be selling to a company, you are first and foremost building a relationship with an individual. That individual has specific needs and challenges and connecting with them on a personal level is necessary so that they know you care about their problem.

LINKEDIN PRO TIP

Why is personalization so powerful?

The psychology behind our need for personalized experiences is relatively easy to understand. Primarily, it can be attributed to two key factors: a desire for control and information overload.[10]

This means that when you know you're getting something that's tailored to your interests, you still perceive having some level of control over what you're engaging with (even when you don't). Personalization also can reduce our perception of information overload.

In short, people prefer personalized content because it is more relevant, and we are naturally more inclined to engage with information that we find relevant and interesting.

Your customers and prospects want to be heard, understood, remembered, and respected. Anything less than this will render you and your business obsolete. Your prospects will look for someone else who "gets" them.

Consider that 63 percent of Millennial consumers and 58 percent of GenX consumers are willing to share their personal data with companies in exchange for personalized offers and discounts.[11] When your messages are targeted to your prospects' unique preferences, your outreach no longer feels like marketing to them. It becomes a smooth interaction with a person or business that "gets" them.

Well-researched personalization is especially critical in your first message—the connection request—with your prospects. You have 300 characters (NOT WORDS) to explain why they should accept your connection request. And the reason you give them must be framed from their perspective, not yours.

Even after your connection request is accepted, you must continue putting in the effort required to create a unique and personalized experience for them with each message you send. Show them your commitment to providing value by only sending them messages and content that are of importance to them.

LINKEDIN PRO STATS[12]

59 percent of customers say that personalization influences their shopping decisions.

31 percent of customers would like their shopping experience to be more personalized than it is.

62 percent of customers are highly in favor of personalized offers/ promotions based on previous experiences.

Look at digital giants Amazon and Netflix; both are famous for placing personalization at the center of their products—programmatically generated "Recommendations for You" are everywhere.

Companies of all sizes and across all industries are discovering the need to make personalization a critical part of their present and future.

The LINK Method™

This image goes a little deeper into The LINK Method™, which starts with Step 1, finding your prospect (covered in the last chapter), and then the specific steps that happen after you have located a potential prospect on LinkedIn.

Figure 6.01

Copyright © TopDogSocialMedia.com

An easy way to remember The LINK Method™, and the steps within it, is with this acronym:

- **L**: Look for prospects and opportunities
- **I**: Initiate a connection
- **N**: Nurture the relationship
- **K**: Kick up the conversation offline

Now that you know how to find prospects on LinkedIn, let's look at the steps that follow to turn a cold prospect into a client.

Each of these steps requires different messages that are a part of The LINK Method™. Doing this right will make you a champion LinkedIn connection and relationship builder. For each message within the sequence, I will help you understand the purpose of the message as well as how to structure each one.

Step 2. Make First Contact

After following Step 1 and finding prospects, it's time to begin the process of connecting. Making first contact starts with sending personalized connection requests to the prospects you've located. The personalized connection request message you send to someone you have never met will, of

course, differ from the ones you'd send to someone you know or even those you've just met. Most of your prospecting will involve connecting with people who you do not know.

This means they don't know you either. These people receive connection requests regularly that are not personalized, and the question they are often asking themselves when receiving a request is, *"Why is this person trying to connect with me?"*

Which brings me to the goal of the connection request message. You must have a personalized message that answers that question, in 300 characters or fewer.

To write a personalized message, start by viewing the person's profile, and see if you can learn what is important to them personally and/or professionally. When writing your request, a great way to begin the message is with something personal to create an immediate connection. It is great when you can find some commonality between you and your prospect.

Your personalized connection request message can be as simple as this:

<Name>,

<Insert something personal or that interested you about person>. <Insert something you share in common>. I'd appreciate the opportunity to connect with you on LinkedIn.

<Your Name>

Or a more specific example would be:

<Name>,

I noticed that you attended <insert school>. I attended the same university, although that seems like a lifetime ago. I enjoy connecting with other alumni and would like an opportunity to connect with you on LinkedIn.

<Your Name>

Your message could mention something you found interesting about them, their profile, their company, or content they've shared:

\<Name\>,

I liked the post you did \<insert what they shared\>. I've looked at your profile, and you have had quite an impressive career. I'd appreciate the opportunity to connect with you on LinkedIn.

\<Your Name\>

When in doubt about what to include in your connection request message, refer to these conversation starters:

- Find commonality
- Comment on something in their profile
- Comment on content they have shared
- Comment on or compliment their company
- Compliment them

Okay, it's your turn. Write down a connection request message you can use when reaching out to new prospects. This can become part of a template you can use and spend seconds adding the personalization.

> **EXERCISE**
> Write down a connection request message you can use when reaching out to new prospects, and keep it under 300 characters.

Don't forget to connect with people you have just or recently met. Perhaps you attended a conference, networking event, or trade fair and met some new people. Connect with them on LinkedIn, where you can begin to nurture that relationship.

In the message you send these people, always remind them of how you met, just in case they have forgotten who you are.

It can be as simple as this example:

Hi <Name>,

It was great to meet you at the <insert event > in <insert location> yesterday, and I would love to connect with you on LinkedIn. If there's anything I can do to support you, please don't hesitate to contact me.

<Your Name>

Be sure to send your message soon after the event where you met; this will increase the likelihood that they will remember you.

Step 3: Engage in Dialogue

Once a prospect has accepted your connection request, your next step is to engage in a dialogue by sending what I call a welcome message or thank you message.

The goal of your welcome message is to establish rapport, start a dialogue, and request nothing in return. Previously, I suggested sending them a link to a helpful resource in the first message. I now recommend that as optional, depending upon who your target market is. Having said that, if you do have a piece of content you think they may appreciate, include it as a P.S. at the bottom.

In this first message, in addition to thanking them for connecting, I suggest you find something to compliment them on. Perhaps ask a question to start a dialogue—if relevant or appropriate—and offer to be a resource to them.

Example of a welcome message including a helpful resource:

<Name>,

Thank you so much for connecting with me.

<Insert compliment about either their profile/professional background/accomplishments, etc.>.

<Ask a question about an initiative in their company or regarding something they shared on LinkedIn in an article or status update>?

If I can be a resource for you with <insert your topic>, please do not hesitate to reach out to me.

<Your Name>

P.S. I have an article you may be interested in; it's called <insert name of article>. You can read it here if this topic is of interest to you: <insert URL>.

Another example without sharing a resource:

<Name>,

Thank you so much for connecting with me.

Congratulations on being recognized as one of the Top 100 Digital Marketing Influencers. I loved the article you recently shared, <insert name of article>. I found it very insightful.

What's next for you at <insert their company name>? Are you working on any exciting projects?

Thanks again for connecting, and if I can be a resource to you, please do not hesitate to reach out to me.

<Your Name>

You never, ever want to pitch anything. The purpose of your welcome message is to begin to build some rapport. If you ask the right question, you can be successful in starting a dialogue with them as well.

Although your welcome message will be 10 times more effective when you take the time to personalize it, you can start to create a template that you can use as the foundation of the messages you send to new connections. It will be a much more efficient process when you have a template that you can then just spend a minute further personalizing.

Okay, it's your turn. Write down a welcome message you can use when reaching out to new prospects.

EXERCISE
Write a welcome message that can be easily adapted with personalization to make this process more efficient for you.

Step 4: Build Relationship

The next message in the sequence is called the relationship-building message, because most people never get past the welcome message. That means they never make further contact or have the chance to build a relationship with their new connection/prospect on LinkedIn. You will typically send this second type of message approximately one week after you send the welcome message.

In this message, you must add value to your new connection/prospect by providing them with a content resource they would find valuable or interesting. The content you share could be your own or content created by someone else. The next chapter will discuss content in-depth, including creating your own content (content creation) or sharing content created by others (content curation), as well as the role it plays in this process.

When deciding what content to share, you must consider these questions: What are they interested in? What is important to them? What problems do they face?

Here is an example of what a relationship-building message may look like:

Hi <Name>,

<Insert a personal statement or question from profile research>.

<Mention the resource you want to share along with a couple of relevant stats or interesting points included in it>.

<Insert a pertinent statement made from the information you pulled in the resource and why it might be helpful or of value to them>.

If you want to check out <insert resource name>, you can find it here: <insert resource URL>.

If you have any questions, or if there is something I can help you with, feel free to reach out to me.

<Your Name>

The resource you offer should be one that specifically relates to helping them overcome a challenge or problem they are having. Again, do NOT pitch anything. Your only goal is to build the relationship, positioning yourself as someone who provides value and is potentially an authority on your topic to increase trust.

Here is a more specific example of what a relationship-building message may look like:

Hi <Name>,

I noticed in your profile that you recently accepted a new position as <insert title> with <insert company> with focus on improving customer engagement for financial institutions.

Congratulations <Name>, that's very exciting!

I've done a lot of work with different financial institutions, and I know that customer engagement is a high priority for them, especially right now.

I recently wrote an article I believe you'll find valuable, it is called <insert name of article>. If you'd like to read it, you can see it here: <insert URL>.

I've had a lot of positive feedback from leaders like yourself. I hope you find it useful.

<Your Name>

Okay, it's your turn once again. Write down what you can send to add value to your new connection/prospect including a resource or something else that they would find valuable or interesting. By taking the time to do this now, you will speed up your social selling process and be much more efficient in attracting new leads and clients. Don't forget to only use this as a template; always spend that one additional minute to personalize it.

> **EXERCISE**
> Write a relationship-building message that can be easily adapted with personalization to make this process more efficient for you.

Step 5: Move Conversation Offline

Since we know the only way to convert a prospect to a client is by moving the conversation offline, that is the next step in this process.

The next message in your sequence will be developed with this purpose in mind, to move the conversation offline. The soonest you would send this message is one week after the last message you sent, the relationship-building message, although you could wait a little longer.

Your goal here is to set up a phone call, video call, or an in-person meeting, depending on how you do business.

Here is an example of what the message to move the conversation offline may look like:

Hi <Name>,

Hope you are doing well.

I was working recently with a client in your industry, and it occurred to me that some of the insights and strategies I helped them with would be highly beneficial to you as well.

Well, that is an assumption of course, as I'm assuming you're interested in improving customer engagement with your clients. Is this even a medium-level priority for you right now?

I'd be happy to share a couple of insights with you over a quick phone call. Do you have 10 minutes free in the next few days?

Let me know a couple of days and times that work for you, and I'd be happy to chat with you.

<Your Name>

It's important to note that if there's been any dialogue that's happened between you and the prospect before this, it alters how you write this message and when you send it. That would include anything they may have previously responded with, especially if it could be incorporated to make your message more relevant and personalized to them.

> **EXERCISE**
> Write a message you can use to move the conversation offline and that can be easily adapted with personalization to make this process more efficient for you.

If you haven't already done the exercises in this chapter, now would be a great time to sit down and do some writing. Once you have some templates written, you will streamline your efforts, save time, and grow a robust network of leads, prospects, and new clients much more efficiently. I recommend you keep these messages in a text document on your computer where you can easily copy and paste the messages and quickly add some personalization.

Here is the complete visual representation of The LINK Method™, revealing the steps, purpose, and timing of each of the messages.

Figure 6.02

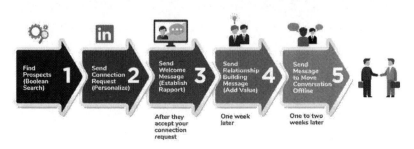

This process isn't going to work with 100 percent of the people you connect with or even 50 percent. There are many factors contributing to why your messages might not generate interest from an individual prospect. Some of them include:

- They are not the right target market
- They don't need what you are offering right now
- They aren't ready for the solution you provide
- It's not a current priority for them
- Personal or professional problems are distracting them
- Or a plethora of other reasons

Not all of your prospects will be ready or motivated by the solution you provide at this point. That doesn't mean that they won't be in six or twelve months from now. I've had many people reach out to me one or two years later. The key is to remain top of mind with these people and not let engagement with them stop at the last message in The LINK Method™.

Which brings me to trigger events you must pay attention to that will provide a comfortable way to re-engage them, even if they've shown no interest at all.

Trigger Events That Provide Engagement Opportunities

In addition to the messages that you send as part of your lead generation sequence, there will also be a number of other reasons when you may want to engage or message your connections. These reasons (also known as trigger events), will provide opportunities to very comfortably and naturally engage your connections, which will allow you to nurture your relationship.

Here are 15 reasons (trigger events) that allow you to engage with or send a message to your connections on LinkedIn comfortably:

1. They viewed your profile
2. You find a prospect you want to connect with
3. Your invitation to connect is accepted
4. Your connection had a job change
5. Your connection got a promotion
6. Your connection mentioned you
7. Your connection updated their profile
8. Your connection liked, commented on, or shared your LinkedIn Publisher post
9. Your connection liked, commented on, or shared your LinkedIn status update
10. Your connection endorsed you
11. You received a recommendation
12. They were mentioned in the news
13. Their company was mentioned in the news
14. They've published an article on LinkedIn
15. They've posted a status update on LinkedIn

In each instance, you want to ensure that your future engagement is still relevant for each person and/or circumstance. The goal is to stay on their radar, provide value, build trust, and eventually be top of mind if they were to want or need the solution you offer.

SOCIAL SELLING PRO TIP

LinkedIn will email you notifications and advise you of a variety of trigger events. For example:

- New Professions and Professional Milestones
- Connections in the News

When you receive these types of messages, look through to see if it represents an ideal opportunity for you to engage with a person identified in these notifications from LinkedIn.

It doesn't end here. There's more gold waiting for you in your network. There's a reason why I have been saying this for years… Your Network = Your Net Worth.

Let's mine your network now for some gold.

Warm Introductions and Referrals

When you have a relationship with someone who knows and trusts you enough to introduce you to someone in their network, take advantage of that opportunity. Why? Buyers are five times more likely to engage with you via a mutual connection (warm referral), and 84 percent of B2B decision makers begin their buying process with a referral.[13]

When asking for an introduction, there is a right way and a wrong way to do this. Unfortunately, most people approach this incredibly valuable process the wrong way, producing either no results or, in some cases, hurting their existing relationship. Remember, you are asking the other person for a favor, so regardless of the outcome, be appreciative and respectful.

To increase your success when requesting an introduction, follow these best practices:

- Build rapport
- Share why you are asking for the introduction
- Make it easy for them
- Give them permission to say no

Warm Introduction Message Process

The message you send will play a considerable role when your connection is considering your request. While you want your message short and to the point, you do want to address these five key points:

1. Establish a personal connection in the first sentence

2. Ask whether or not they know someone well enough to provide an introduction

3. Let them know that you will provide the message to send so they don't have any extra work to make the introduction

4. Show appreciation for their time, and thank them in advance

5. Offer to return the favor if there is anyone they want to meet in your network.

Example

Hi <Referrer Name>,

I hope all is well with you. <Insert a personal statement or question from profile research>.

I notice that you are connected to <Referral First and Last Name> on LinkedIn, and I was wondering if you know <her/him> well enough to make an introduction. If you do, I'd really appreciate it if you can do a quick intro.

I'll even write a short introduction note (in a separate message), so you don't have to spend more than a minute on this.

I appreciate any assistance you can offer. Of course, if I can ever introduce you to anyone in my network, please don't hesitate to ask.

<Your Name>

They Said No

If they say no, send them a polite message. It could be as simple as this:

Hi <Name>,

Not a problem, I thought it was worth a shot. Thanks for getting back to me. Have a great day.

<Your Name>

They Said Yes. Now Send Your Follow-Up Message

If your connection agrees to your request, you will need to follow up with a message and thank them for their help, including a short sample message they can send to the person they are introducing you to. You are asking them for a favor; you don't want to put all the work on their shoulders. Also, by taking this extra step, you not only make it easier for them, but they are also much more likely to follow through with your request. Here are five important points to include in your follow-up message:

1. Thank contact for agreeing to make an introduction
2. Provide a simple message that is easy for them to send
3. Include third-party credibility
4. Make the reason for the introduction clear
5. Encourage the referral to make contact

Sample Referral Follow-Up Message Template

Hi <Referrer Name>,

Thank you so much for agreeing to introduce me to <Referral Name>. I wanted to make this super easy for you, so I have included a message below that you can easily copy, paste, and send. Of course, feel free to edit it as you see fit.

Hi <Referral Name>,

I hope all is well with you. I'd like to introduce you to <Your First and Last Name>, <insert statement of how you have previously helped the person making the introduction or something about your relationship with them>. <Insert the reason for the introduction>. <Insert encouragement for the referral to reach out to you>.

I'll leave it to the two of you to take it from here.

<Referrer Name>

<Your Name>

It's that simple to mine your network for warm introductions and referrals. So, what are you waiting for? Oh yes, wait until you have a profile you can be proud of. If you haven't done that yet, then make sure you do this before you start prospecting or asking for introductions.

Let's recap what you learned in this chapter. You learned The LINK Method™ of how to find a prospect, create a connection, and move that conversation offline. You also learned how to look for trigger events that will allow you to continue to engage with and nurture prospects that didn't move to an offline conversation. Additionally, you now know how to ask for warm introductions and mine your network for gold.

Mapping this out may seem overwhelming. To give you an overview and a process to follow, be sure to **download the FREE companion workbook** at http://LinkedInUnlockedWorkbook.com

It's time to move on to creating content that will allow you to stay top of mind with your network of prospects and position yourself as an authority.

CHAPTER SEVEN

THE CONTENT MARKETING ROADMAP

Content marketing allows you to move beyond just someone trying to sell something to a trusted authority on your topic.

It takes time and work to build authority, credibility, and trust, but the benefits you receive will be worth the investment.

One of the easiest ways to build authority, credibility, and trust is by creating and sharing content that is valuable to your ideal clients. Within three months of creating content and leveraging LinkedIn, I became known as an authority in my community and was asked to speak at numerous local events. Seven years ago, no one knew me outside of this community.

Today, I travel extensively across North America and Europe, and people know me in every city and country I travel to. That didn't happen merely because of social media. That happened because of the content I share across social media, which people find helpful to their businesses.

When you are perceived as a trusted authority, you become the first choice in the minds of potential prospects when they look for the solution to their problem(s). This is because they now know, like, and trust you, as you have demonstrated the expertise that proves you can help them solve their challenge or problem.

So, just how do you prove your expertise and help your prospects?

Through the **ACT** of content marketing, which over time will increase Authority, Credibility, and Trust.

Figure 7.01

CONTENT MARKETING ACT ™

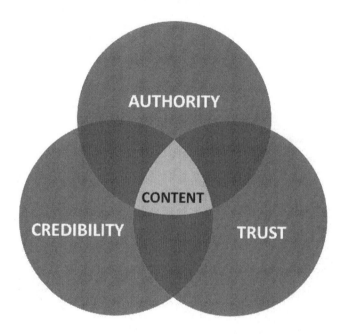

AUTHORITY

CONTENT

CREDIBILITY

TRUST

Copyright © 2018 | Top Dog Social Media

Content marketing is creating and distributing relevant and valuable content to attract, acquire, and engage a defined target audience—with the objective of driving profitable customer action.

The content you share can be your original content or curated content. Curating content is sharing content created by others that would be of value to your target audience.

Types of Content

Content can take many forms. It can be written, audio, video, or visual.

Let me provide some examples of the different types of content you could create:

Written content: blog posts, articles, guest blog posts, whitepapers, eBooks, reports, case studies, emails, surveys, etc.

Audio content: podcasts, interviews, expert interviews, Q&A sessions, FAQs, etc.

Video content: how to's, product demos, testimonials, Q&A sessions, webinars, live streams, vlogs, etc.

Visual content: infographics, images, SlideShare presentations, charts, graphs, quotes, checklists, etc.

LINKEDIN PRO STAT

A LinkedIn survey found that B2B buyers are five times more likely to engage with a sales professional who provides content with new insights about their business or industry.[14]

To be successful with your content, you need to understand your ideal client's problems, which you already identified in the exercises in Chapter 2. Your goal in using content is to educate your ideal clients on the solution(s) to solve their problem or challenge.

Your success will also depend on the quality of the content you are sharing. You need to ensure that everything you share is high-value from the perspective of your ideal client. What you consider high-value and what they believe is high-value may be different.

High-value content that inspires engagement should be:

• High-quality

• Educational

- Solution based
- Timely and relevant
- Non-promotional
- Engaging and/or entertaining

There's no better or faster way to build your authority than through creating and sharing high-value content.

Creating Original Content

To build authority, you must create and share original content. There are many good reasons for this, but the most important is to establish thought leadership and be seen as a trusted resource on your topic.

Some other benefits include increasing your visibility, driving more traffic to your website, building the size of your email list, getting found organically in web search results, more opportunities for engagement with prospects, and developing the critical *know, like,* and *trust* factors.

There is a lot of research to support the value of taking the time to create original content.

82 percent of consumers feel MORE positive about a company after reading custom content, and 90 percent find custom content useful.

In fact, 60 percent of people are inspired to seek out a product after reading content about it.[15]

Additional research suggests 65 percent of buyers feel that the vendor's content had an impact on their final purchase decision and that nearly 82 percent of buyers viewed five to eight pieces of content from a winning vendor.[16]

Content Marketing Roadmap: The B2B Buyer's Journey

So how do you know which kind of content to provide to which members of your target market?

It's simple. Know and understand the buyer's journey.

The buyer's journey is a structured process that shows you the different stages the potential buyer finds himself or herself themselves in depending on their level of knowledge and need at any given moment.

Mapping the B2B Buyer's Journey

Every B2B buyer's journey starts with a problem. That's what will prompt them to find a solution. We call this a pain point, and an individual or an entire company may experience it.

This is where the search for a solution begins. The person or company suffering from the problem starts to look for as much content as possible to figure out the different solutions available. After taking a look at the advantages and disadvantages presented by each potential solution, they will decide which one would work best for their specific needs.

Stages of the B2B Buyer's Journey

Figure 7.02

Content Marketing Roadmap: The B2B Buyer's Journey

Awareness	Consideration	Decision	Retention	Advocacy
GET TRAFFIC	GET LEADS	GET SALES	RETAIN & REFERRALS	ADVOCATE
• Social Media Updates • Infographics • Digital Magazine • Audio Podcast • Newsletter • Blog • Microsite • Video	• Educational Resources • Software Download • Quiz / Survey • Webinar • Events • Discount / Coupon • Useful Resource	• Demo / FREE Trial • Case Studies • Comparison / Spec Sheet • Webinar • Event • Mini-Class • Quotes / Estimates	• Demo / FREE Trial • Email / Newsletters • FREE Consultations • Quotes / Estimates • Blog • Video • Audio Podcast	• Email / Newsletters • Social Media Updates • Audio Podcast • Video • Webinar • Blog

The content marketing roadmap provides a framework that you can use to guide your content efforts, based on your objectives at each stage.

1. The Awareness Stage: Use Content Marketing to Get Noticed and Obtain Web Traffic

The first stage of the buyer's journey involves getting people to see and read your content.

The people you want to attract are looking for answers, so the kind of content you should provide at this stage must be focused on that. Your goal here is to inform them about the best ways to solve their problems.

The relevant types of content for the awareness stage are:

- **Newsletters and email marketing**: Keep in touch regularly with your subscribers with newsletters and email marketing campaigns

- **White papers**: Pull out all of your expertise and convert that into well-written and compelling white papers

- **Blog posts**: Blog posts are also helpful at this stage because they're easily digestible and can be informative at the same time

- **Checklists and tip sheets**: Other types of content that work well at this stage are checklists and tip sheets

- **Infographics**: Visual content like infographics are excellent choices for effective sharing of information

- **Social media updates**: You can also use social media updates with links to your content to generate traffic and awareness

Remember that the ideal approach here is to offer these resources for free. You'd be hard-pressed to find people willing to pay you for information that they can quickly get elsewhere. Set aside that financial goal for now, and focus on the fact that your objective is to inform and assist, not make a profit from the get-go.

2. The Consideration Stage: Develop a Content Marketing Strategy for Getting Leads and Keeping Them

The potential buyers at this stage already know what you can offer them to address their pain points; your goal now is to build your credibility further and infuse your content with opportunities to reach out and engage with your audience on a more personal level.

The relevant types of content for the consideration stage are:

- **Webinars, live streaming, and live events**: These are a popular way to demonstrate your expertise on a particular subject

- **Case studies**: You can publish case studies that talk about the benefits that working with you can offer, or even an objective comparison between you and your competitors to show potential buyers what makes you unique

- **Reviews and testimonials**: You can use reviews and testimonials to demonstrate social proof, enhancing your credibility to potential buyers

- **Social selling**: You can incorporate social selling at this stage to gain further interest from potential buyers

- **LinkedIn lead generation**: LinkedIn is also particularly useful at this stage to generate leads

3. The Decision Stage: Focus Your Content Strategy on Getting Sales

This is the selling point—the part you've been carefully building up to with all your content offers. If you have set things up correctly in the earlier stages, you should be reaping the benefits now.

One thing to remember is that you have to be patient. Most prospective buyers need to get through three out of the five stages before they are ready to think about buying.

In this stage, the relevant types of content for the decision stage are:

- **Free trials, consultations, assessment, quotes/proposals, and demos**: You can share free trials and demos with potential buyers, invite them to request a quote from you, or even offer free consultations to get them moving along on their journey

- **Sales conversations**: At this stage, you can also get on the phone or meet in person to have a conversation to discuss how your solution will solve the buyer's problem and increase their confidence in your product or service

4. The Retention Stage: Incorporate Retention and Referrals into Your Content Marketing Strategy

After making a sale, don't leave your customer behind. This is the stage where you need to continue to be present for them. This is the perfect time to make them feel they are an important part of your community.

The relevant types of content for the retention stage are:

- **Email marketing**: Implement email campaigns that get your new customer acquainted with your other products, and continue to educate and nurture them

- **Social media updates**: Develop a consistent social media management strategy

- **Live streaming and videos**: Send them emails announcing when you're doing some live streaming or you've uploaded a new video

- **Blog posts**: Publish a new blog post at least once a week

- **Case studies**: Organize case studies, and make sure they are up-to-date

- **Podcasts**: Podcasts are also a great way to create a voice for your brand that your customers can listen to

5. The Advocacy Stage: Develop Your Loyal Customers into Brand Advocates

Developing loyalty provides third-party credibility, referrals, and introductions. There are four relevant types of content for the advocacy stage:

1. **Warm introductions and referrals**: Maintain relationships with your customers, and notice with whom they are connected. The third-party credibility you get from receiving a warm introduction goes a long way in accelerating the sales process.

2. **Social media engagement**: Watch what your customers and prospects post online; don't miss an opportunity to like, comment, or share their posts when relevant. Their connections are able to see your posts, and that opens you up to their network.

3. **Social sharing of content**: Make sure that your content is easily shareable. Add social sharing options to your website and all other content. Your biggest advocates will share your content often; make sure this is easy for them to do.

4. **Webinars**: Continue to add value to your existing customers by offering an educational webinar series, and allow them to invite others to it.

Remember the buyer's journey is a step-by-step process that requires more than just a one-size-fits-all content marketing strategy. When it comes to planning and creating content, putting in that extra effort to offer your audience what they need will make all the difference. It is also imperative that it is professional looking. If you cannot produce professional-level content, stick to curating other's content or hire someone to do it for you.

Curating Content

Curating and sharing other's content is an essential part of your content marketing strategy, whether or not you are creating original content of your own.

Curating content is beneficial to you because:

- Providing information that is of interest or helpful to your prospects on related topics that you are not an authority on actually further increases your credibility and increases trust

- When posting other's content with the addition of your perspective, you create more opportunities for discussion and engagement with prospects

- You create the chance to build relationships with experts in related areas, potentially providing partnership opportunities and the ability to expand the reach of your original content

- Sharing other's content is more efficient than just creating your own original content while also allowing you to share fresh insights with your prospects regularly

- Curating content helps your prospects, which is ultimately your goal—and this helps to strengthen and build your relationships

Content Curation Best Practices

With curated content, just how can your strategy make you stand out, given that there are over 4.48 billion pages indexed on the web at the time of this writing?

Here are some content curation best practices:

Add Your Perspective

Don't take existing content and only share a link to it. Put some effort in, and personalize it. You can simply add quotes or insights from within the curated content, or, preferably, you can share your perspective on the content you're sharing.

Anybody can cut and paste content; anyone can share a link. Your prospects can find that anywhere. What they want is your unique perspective. They want to know what you think or feel about what you are sharing. It's your perspective that will differentiate your curation from people who simply share a link. For maximum impact, be sure to include your perspective and insights when you are sharing curated content.

Engage with Your Audience: Ask Questions, Respond to Comments, and Show Them Your Human Side

It's also not enough to keep sharing links to articles with your audience. That's like starting a conversation without bothering to continue it. Occasionally ask a question so that you can better understand what they think or feel about specific topics, and then respond to their answers to show them that their opinions and input matter to you.

Include a CTA

Sharing curated content without a proper call-to-action (CTA) is a missed opportunity to get your audience to take a particular action. Your CTA may be as simple as asking them to read the article and share their thoughts or to take some other action. People are more likely to take action when you tell them explicitly the action you want them to take.

It's important to note that you should also include a CTA when you share your original content.

How to Find Content to Share

There are many places online where you can find really good content to share. Start with looking at reputable publications in your industry as a source for content.

There is so much content published that it can be hard to keep up. You can attempt to do this manually and check multiple sites and sources every day, but this can become a severe time drain. Instead, you could use a news aggregator application such as Feedly that will compile newsfeeds from a variety of online sources, ones that you have personally added. By using a tool such as this, you can quickly find content from sources you trust, without having to scour the web.

You can also set up Google Alerts on terms and topics you want to monitor.

Another excellent source is the newsfeed on your LinkedIn home page. Here you will find a wide variety of relevant content shared from your network and influencers you follow, which you can share directly from the newsfeed as a status update.

If you're using Twitter, it can be useful to quickly and easily find content from great sources to share. Your sources can be industry publications, businesses, organizations, or individuals, as long as they consistently post quality content. Create Twitter lists of these sources to quickly see the most recent posts from your list of trusted content sources. You can also search Twitter for popular topics, hashtags, or your chosen keywords. Pay attention to the tweets that are getting the most retweets and favorites, as this is ideal content for you to share.

You should also check out the website and newsletters from your favorite brands, industry organizations, and influencers.

LINKEDIN PRO EXERCISE

Create a separate folder in your email where you can save all the newsletters and emails you receive from industry experts and influencers that your ideal clients could potentially be interested in, whether they are in your area of expertise or other related areas of interest.

Each week go through these emails, and look for high-quality content that you can share on LinkedIn and any other relevant social channels. Don't forget to include your perspective and ask questions occasionally to encourage engagement.

Content Curation Tools

Here's a list of some of my favorite content curation tools:

Feedly

One of my favorite tools, Feedly offers two options when it comes to content curation. You can visit one site at a time, grab the URL, and paste it where you'll be sharing it. Your other option is news aggregation, which merely involves adding your favorite sources of news to your account. This will enable you to browse these feeds from just one device via Feedly.

Storify

Storify allows users to search for the top stories on social media sites and choose which ones to turn into stories or use as content. Storify may seem a bit challenging to use at first, but it is worth mastering.

Owler

Owler is a business insights platform that delivers curated content about your industry straight to your inbox. You may choose from its three offerings, depending on which suits your needs best: the bite-sized Instant Insights, a day's worth of content compiled as a Daily Snapshot, and the week's best presented under Weekly Showdown.

Google Alerts

No content curation tools list is complete without Google Alerts. This tool allows you to set up multiple alerts about anything from your brand, industry, or competitors—giving you a glimpse of the conversations happening about your chosen keyword(s) and who's talking about them.

Google Alerts will send you notifications via email whenever it's able to match an alert you've set. You can also set multiple alerts to keep track of more than a single topic at a given time.

A word of caution: Always take the time to read through any content you are going to share to make sure that it is high-quality content and relevant to your audience. Just as high-quality content can help your credibility, so too can irrelevant or poor content hurt it.

I could have created a much more extensive list of tools, as there's an endless list, but I believe less is more. Fewer tools, fewer tasks, less overwhelm.

Best Practices with Content Marketing on LinkedIn

Content marketing cannot be underestimated and is a crucial part of building authority, credibility, and trust and attracting leads and prospects to you. Let me wrap up with some of the best practices you should use when using LinkedIn.

Reach Out to More People Through High-Quality, Long-Form Content

One of LinkedIn's most popular and useful features is the ability to draft and publish long-form content on the platform via LinkedIn Publisher. This feature functions similarly to the blog feature on your website with the added benefit of showcasing your latest Publisher posts right within your profile. This enables you to educate any leads, prospects, and clients that visit your profile. Each time someone likes, comments, or shares your articles on LinkedIn Publisher, their network will also see it, opening you up to a much wider audience.

Share Content on Status Updates

Share your own and other's content consistently to keep you top of mind and position you as an authority on your topic with your connections. Follow these best practices for sharing content:

- **Offer newsworthy content and updates**: You can share news updates related to your industry from credible sources. You can also provide updates to your followers about the latest events at your company.

- **Ask relevant questions of your target audience**: Ask your followers about their thoughts, opinions, or experience on a specific issue. Questions have power.

- **Provide compelling storytelling**: Tell a story that gives your followers more insight into you. Your updates must be compelling and must share information with your audience in an interesting way.

- **Have a healthy mix of content topics and formats**: Don't be afraid to mix it up and keep your audience interested. You can share content on a wide variety of topics (from personal to business), with different voices (from inspirational to aspirational) and storytelling techniques (text updates, visual marketing, and images).

- **Offer content, updates, and messages that trigger an emotional response**: Share content, updates, and messages that can make your audience feel a strong emotional response. This must be done cautiously in a business setting.

- **Include a call-to-action**: If you want people to take a specific action, tell them what that action is. As much as possible, be direct without being too blunt or sounding desperate. If you want people to comment, invite them to comment, but provide something substantial for them to comment on in the first place.

Send Helpful Content Directly to Prospects Through Personalized Messages

Become a resource for answers and knowledge for your hottest prospects by sending them content that is of specific interest to them, which solves their problems and helps them overcome their challenges. Tailor your approach according to the individual and on information from their LinkedIn profile. This keeps you top of mind and builds trust.

Establish Authority on Your Topic with Video Content

Many people respond well to video content. Video humanizes you and allows people to get to know you more intimately. Besides, it is one of the best ways to establish authority on your topic and in your niche. People relate to video, and science shows that the brain is hard-wired to trust the human face.

Incorporate LinkedIn Video

Did you know that 60 percent of B2B marketers use some form of online video within their overall marketing strategy?[17]

As stated above, there is also plenty of science to back up the use of video, which has proven that the human voice conveys emotion, and that movement captures and keeps people's attention. Also, the human brain is hardwired to trust the human face. Each of these is a great reason why you need to consider adding video to your strategy if you haven't already.

LINKEDIN PRO STATS[18]

79 percent of consumers agree video is the easiest way to get to know a brand online.

First and foremost, nearly three-quarters (74 percent) of consumers pointed to a connection between watching a video on social media and their purchasing decision-making process. In fact, roughly half (46 percent) of consumers said they have made a purchase as a result of watching a brand video on social media, and another third (32 percent) have considered doing so.

Thankfully, when it comes to innovation, being first isn't a prerequisite for being the best. LinkedIn was last to add a native video feature. LinkedIn video offers incredible relationship-building possibilities. You can upload and share videos directly from your mobile phone, allowing your network to enjoy unique and original video content that's relevant and of interest to them.

You are also able to see how well your videos are performing; you can check the number of views they're getting (defined as any instance wherein the video is played for longer than three seconds) as well as the level of engagement your videos receive.

Just like everything else you do on LinkedIn, you need to be strategic in posting videos to LinkedIn and include best practices such as:

- Start with the most critical information at the beginning of your video

- Keep your video to under two minutes, preferably one minute

- Be relevant in your message; do your research

- Include a CTA (call-to-action)

Content Marketing Strategy

At this point, you know that content marketing involves creating, distributing, and sharing content to engage audiences, generate leads, and improve branding, which leads to building authority, credibility, and trust. To accomplish this, your content marketing will require a strategic approach.

This starts with defining the specific vision and goals you have for content marketing and then creating *audience personas* (begin with the ideal client descriptions you created earlier), *content maps* (the content marketing roadmap), *your brand story* (your why story expanded), and *a channel plan* (a plan for how you will use each publishing channel, e.g., social media, newsletter, website, etc.). Once you have this outlined, you can go on to create a content marketing calendar and action plan to keep you focused and organized.

The content calendar and action plan you create will depend on your:

- Size of business
- Time
- Budget
- Goals

A solo professional services provider who must do all the tasks to run their business will have a very different plan than a company with a dedicated marketing professional or team.

Regardless of the size of your business or organization, you must determine how much time you will allow for the person(s) responsible for carrying out your plan.

This needs to be reasonable and achievable; otherwise, your plan will not be followed. You may think that you want to dedicate two hours a day to content creation and curation, but if you cannot realistically spend that much time at it, you need to determine what you can be consistent with.

The more aggressive your goals, and the more platforms you use, the more time you will need to spend on your content marketing efforts.

You also need to determine what kind of budget you have to dedicate to content marketing. There's been a big myth for years that content marketing is FREE. I have not ever seen anyone be truly successful at content marketing without allocating a budget to it.

Your content marketing budget will need to include things such as:

- Content creation (i.e., if you outsource a content writer, editor, graphic designer to create graphics, etc.)

- Social media scheduling and analytic tools (e.g., Agorapulse, Sprout Social, Buffer, etc.)

- Social ads to boost your reach (e.g., Facebook or LinkedIn advertising)

- The time that you or your team can spend on implementation, content creation, content curation, engagement, prospecting, outreach, etc.

Finally, you need to decide which of the identified goals you are going to start with. If you are a one-person show, you may want to only choose one or two goals to begin with.

I suggest you start with the goals that will provide you with the quickest wins. This is why I focus so much attention on LinkedIn and showing my clients how to implement The LINK Method™. It always creates the fastest wins.

Implementing Your Content Marketing Strategy

There can be no results without effective implementation of your content marketing strategy. The more aspects of your social selling that you have documented, the more efficient the entire process will become.

Create a content marketing checklist documenting the activities you will do and the frequency.

These activities can include:

- Creating content (writing blog posts, producing videos, etc.)

- Curating content (reviewing industry websites, RSS feeds, Google alerts, etc.)

- Outsourcing tasks (e.g., having professional graphics designed, etc.)

- Editing and uploading blog posts and articles

- Sharing content

- Engaging with comments on your content

Create a document, and outline all of the tasks by how often they are to be done, in chronological order (daily, weekly, monthly).

Sort each of these tasks in order of importance with the most critical tasks at the top.

It's helpful to go into even more detail and list the specific activities for each day of the week. For example, your Thursday items might include posting an article to LinkedIn Publisher, and your Monday items involve writing a blog post.

Once you have created your checklist, use it every day. Check off each task as you complete it.

Content Publishing Calendar

If you are creating original content, you need to create a content calendar.

This is very beneficial, as you won't be left trying to think of a topic to write about the day before you plan to publish a post.

Your calendar should include things like:

- Post date

- Ideal client the content targets (if you have more than one)

- Challenge it addresses

- Title

- Focus keyword

- CTA

If you have a team, you might want to include who is writing and editing the content and any due dates as well.

Try to plan your content calendar for two months to one year in advance. You can be flexible and make changes to it from time to time if you need to address an issue that is timely and relevant.

CHAPTER EIGHT

ELEVATING AUTHORITY, CREDIBILITY, AND TRUST

It is a fundamental truth that people buy from people they ***know, like,*** and ***trust.*** To accomplish this, you need to build relationships based on trust and establish your authority on your topic.

Trust: *Assured reliance on the character, ability, strength, or truth of someone or something; one in which confidence is placed.*

In the last chapter, I discussed the vital role content marketing has in developing authority, credibility, and trust. This topic deserves an entire chapter because establishing authority, credibility, and trust with your prospects is crucial to successfully moving your relationship to a place where you can take it offline and ultimately have a sales conversation.

The LINK Method™ is all about building relationships with your prospects, and it is much easier to do that when you are perceived as someone knowledgeable and credible. It is harder to gain trust in the digital world, where you don't get the chance to meet someone eye to eye. For that reason, you need to find digital ways to help prospects get to know, like, and trust you.

Over time, your content will be seen and recognized by others, possibly influencers or others in your industry. This can result in many opportunities for you to get in front of a brand-new audience. If you are creating high-value content, you may be asked to provide articles for industry publications, be a guest blogger on a well-known site, or be interviewed in a webinar or podcast.

Each of these presents fantastic opportunities for you to leverage third-party credibility from people who, themselves, have a loyal community. For example, in the past week, I have $18,000 in sales just from a webinar I did for someone else's audience. I didn't sell anything in the webinar; I simply educated their audience, and some people reached out to me to find out how I could help them.

I was asked by a well-known marketer two years ago if he could interview me on his podcast. That podcast continues to be listened to and has generated tens of thousands of dollars in business for me. Again, I didn't offer anything for sale during the podcast interview.

I talk a lot about the need to build relationships and move conversations offline so you can get to know a prospect better and ultimately position what you offer as a solution to their problems. I also say that sales don't happen until you get to that step—an offline conversation.

Is that always the case?

In the past week, two people have bought LinkedIn-related services that I offer without ever having talked to me. In both cases, they asked me one question via email, I answered, and they bought. This could never have happened if they didn't see me as an authority on LinkedIn, know that I was credible, and believe that they could trust me.

In this chapter I want to share some additional ways beyond content marketing that you can increase authority, credibility, and trust in the eyes of your prospects and clients and also with peers, influencers, and others.

Build a Community

If you remember back to the introduction of this book, it was my community (social media friends, connections, followers) that was responsible for helping me find my father, whom I had never met. It was because of them that my video went viral and was picked up by the media, which resulted in worldwide coverage of my story. It even led to someone creating a Wikipedia page for me.

Also, every single time I create a new piece of content, many people in my community share it with their communities, opening me up to a much larger audience, one I may not have been able to reach on my own.

What better way to help people know, like, and trust you than to create a community of engaged members? The members of your community will be most engaged when they trust and respect you, feel a sense of belonging, and know that you care about what's important to them.

Here are the three essential elements you must include when building a community that will be engaged and want and need what you offer:

1. Be Real

Allow people to see the real you.

Being authentic is essential if you want people to get to know you, like you, and trust you.

Admittedly, this used to be very hard for me. It was easy for me to talk about business related topics, add value through content, and never let anyone know anything personal about me.

Remember the video of me sharing the story of how I had never met my father? It was one of the hardest things I had to do—to fully expose myself in such a vulnerable way. But in doing so, not only did my community rush in to help me, they got to know me more intimately and connected with me on a deeper level.

This doesn't mean oversharing. There is a line that should not be crossed because it borders the realm of oversharing, and this line is different depending on the platform you are on and, of course, your industry.

So, how do you allow people to see the real you when posting business related materials on LinkedIn? Use your own voice. Don't be afraid to let your personality shine in your posts and content. It is important though that your voice is consistent over all of your platforms and content. This is what will attract others with similar goals or beliefs as you.

Remember that people want to know your perspective. So, share it with them when you are sharing content. When relevant, add a story about why you have that perspective.

2. Engage

A community is not possible without conversation and engagement.

As it relates to LinkedIn (or other social networks), sharing posts and never engaging with the people who leave comments is merely broadcasting, not community- or relationship-building.

While you may be accustomed to speaking *at* your audience with your content and sales materials, this does nothing to support or build your community. Real relationships require give and take from both sides, and conversations and engagement need two-way communication.

This requires you to listen and respond to your community members, when and where they are communicating with you.

As you listen and respond, take cues on what they are sharing with you. Often, you will find vital information contained within their messages. This information provides additional insights into their needs or challenges and gives you essential information for future content and products or services.

CONTENT MARKETING PRO TIP

Not sure what your next article or video should be? Review the recent engagement and conversations with your community for ideas and suggestions.

There are many places where your community can communicate with you on LinkedIn. This could be on your status updates, under comments you've made on other people's posts, LinkedIn Publisher posts, group posts, your content that someone has shared, or in a private LinkedIn message. Their interaction can take the form of likes, comments, shares, and/or messages.

If someone takes the time to comment (good or bad), it is vital that you reply as soon as possible.

You may also find opportunities to interact with your LinkedIn community outside of LinkedIn, on the other social media platforms they are using. For example, many LinkedIn users are also active on Twitter, but this may or may not be relevant in your industry or with your ideal clients.

TWITTER PRO TIP

If you are using Twitter, create one or more Twitter lists with people (prospects, clients, peers, influencers) who you'd like to engage with on that platform.

3. Provide Value

Ensure that in every interaction with your community, you are providing them with value.

Always ask yourself, *"What's in it for them?"*

People view everything through their *WIIFM* filter (*what's in it for me?*) when they are looking at your content. Think about it from their perspective. If there is no clear benefit for them, then they won't waste their time because there is so much competing for their time and attention.

Whatever you do, do not bombard your community with your sales and marketing messages and materials. This is the quickest way to destroy the relationship that you are working to build.

Once you have an engaged community that you consistently add value to, through both your content and interactions, you will become the first person they think about if they need your solution, as a result of increased authority, credibility, and trust. More importantly, if anyone in their network is looking for the solution you offer, you will be the first person they recommend to their contacts.

Collaborate

One of the fastest ways to expand your network and community is through collaborating with others. As I mentioned earlier in this chapter, this is a fantastic opportunity to leverage the third-party credibility that comes from being recommended by others.

But there's no need to wait for that to happen passively. There are proactive steps you can take in building relationships with people through collaboration that provide a win-win-win. A win for you when they refer you, a win for them when you refer them, and a win for the prospect that either of you is helping. After all, business should always be a win-win-win.

Below are a few essential elements of collaboration on LinkedIn. These will help you build trust with your connections, expand the size of your community, and establish your authority on your topic.

1. Take the Initiative

The chance to help your connections will not always come, so don't wait for opportunities to collaborate or help them—*create* opportunities.

This is especially important if you are working to build your authority on your topic.

Look for collaboration opportunities with other professionals or influencers who provide complementary products or services. An example of this might be interviewing someone on a topic that would be of interest to your target market and introducing them to your community. That interview could be shared in a blog post, podcast, video, live stream, or webinar.

As well as aiding your connections by introducing them to someone who can help them (in an area that you don't work in), there is also the chance to be introduced to the connections and community of the person you are collaborating with. This is a fantastic way to expand your reach and gain credibility.

Collaborative opportunities can take many additional forms, including:

Strategic Alliance: This is when two or more people/companies work together to pursue an agreed upon goal while remaining independent of each other. For example, if you work with another expert to co-run a podcast, create a training program, or create a live streaming show.

Joint Venture Partner (JVP): This is when two or more people/companies come together to form a temporary partnership to complete a specific event or project. For example, when a group of related experts gets together to run an online summit or conference, or share someone's program to your email list (affiliate relationship) where they can earn an affiliate commission for any sales generated.

Referral Partner: This is a person or company that sends relevant prospective leads to you and you to them because you offer complementary services to similar audiences. For example, if you're an accountant, you might set up a referral partnership with a business attorney.

COLLABORATION PRO EXERCISE

Set a goal to find and approach at least one potential collaborative partner a month.

2. Be a Connector

When you see an opportunity to help your connections grow their network or business, do some business matchmaking when you can. Again, this represents a win-win-win. The third win, in this case, is that if the two people you connect end up helping each other, they will always remember that you made the introduction.

Such an act will also invoke reciprocity. Nothing makes a stronger and more genuine impression than when you give selflessly, generously, and (most importantly) without the expectation of receiving anything in return. This good deed has a high potential of being reciprocated when the people you introduced come across someone they think can benefit from being introduced to you.

This brings up third-party credibility again when someone who knows and trusts you introduces you to someone else. There's a much higher degree of trust right from the start.

When introducing two of your connections, send them a message letting them know why you think each would benefit from knowing the other.

NETWORKING PRO EXERCISE

Start being a connector right now. Find two people in your network you can introduce who could benefit in some way from getting to know each other.

Get Committed

What does commitment have to do with LinkedIn or social selling?

Random actions will not have the same impact as those that are planned out in advance, carried out on a consistent basis, and that people can trust will continue. You must be committed to succeed at social selling.

Jean-Paul Sartre summed this up perfectly when he said, *"Commitment is an act, not a word."*

For me, commitment means that my community knows they can depend on me to create valuable content for them (blog posts, videos, newsletters, books, courses, etc.) that will help them be more successful with their business. I prove that commitment to them by consistently sharing my best knowledge, resources, and systems with them.

Here are the three essential elements you need to be committed to, which will help you attract the right people to your network, further increase your authority on your subject matter, and firmly establish the trust of your community:

1. Intention

You must know and understand what your intentions are (your WHY) to be truly successful in elevating your authority, credibility, and the trust your community (or network) has in you.

People can quickly sense when your intention is self-serving, and this will repel people. Conversely, the opposite is also true; you will attract those people to you who resonate with your core intention or commitment. These are the people who want and need what you are offering.

If you do not understand your intentions, your community will not either. Your messages will turn out inauthentic, and that will severely limit your ability to establish trust and generate sales.

2. Time

Be committed to being consistent.

Consistency requires a time commitment. Time is scarce for all of us; we only have so many hours in the day. So, you need to determine how much time you can set aside each day, week, and month to commit to creating and sharing content, engaging with your community, prospecting, and then following up with the messages in The LINK Method™ to build relationships and gain more clients.

Be realistic.

You are better to set aside too much time than too little. If you have less time than planned, you're more likely to skip or procrastinate with your social selling activities. The most important thing is that you stick to whatever schedule you have set up and remain consistent.

In the beginning, it will take you longer to implement the social selling activities in this book. After you get more comfortable and confident, things will move along much more efficiently.

3. Trust

Increase your authority and credibility, and the outcome is trust.

I wrote a quote that has been shared tens of thousands of times because it resonates with people. I'd like to share it with you:

> *People don't care about your business.*
> *They care about their problems.*
> *Be the solution they are looking for.*

But there's something that's missing from the quote in the context of building trust. This brings me to another of my favorite quotes, which is:

> **People *won't* care how much you know**
> ***until* they know *how* much you care.**

People will trust you when they know you can provide the solution they need and that you care about them or their business. No matter how skilled you are, if they can't see that you care, they won't do business with you.

The next step in elevating your authority, credibility, and trust is showing a sufficient amount of social proof.

Social Proof

Social proof is one of the key influencers that people use when making a decision about with whom to do business. People look to what others have done when making a decision, and that's why reviews, testimonials, and endorsements have been so influential for businesses.

The Social Proof Theory, made famous by psychologist Robert Cialdini, states that a person who does not know what the proper behavior for a particular situation is will look to other people to imitate what they are doing and to guide their actions. In simpler terms, social proof helps us make decisions when we are uncertain, based on the experiences and choices others make or have made in the past.

People tend to base their decisions on the reactions and decisions of their peers. Nobody wants to be the guinea pig. It's nice to be able to gain wisdom through the second-hand experiences of those we trust.

Even the size of your network can exhibit a form of social proof, especially in specific industries. For example, I had met a man who wanted to promote himself as a social media marketing consultant, helping businesses with social media. I looked at his social profiles, he had 77 followers on Twitter and 352 connections on LinkedIn.

I asked him, *"How are you going to help people with social media when you don't seem to know how to grow your following?"*

He replied saying, *"Well do you think you could teach me?"*

My answer was a resounding, *"NO."* I did not want to be responsible for unleashing another unqualified marketer who would take money from businesses and provide no results.

In the world of marketing, a level of social proof is evident by the following you have. I'm consistently amazed at companies in the marketing industry that have practically a non-existent audience.

Consider this: Would you hire a marketing consultant who has two recommendations on their LinkedIn profile over one who has over 100 recommendations?

Do you think the number of recommendations would have an impact on a potential prospect?

According to the proven theory of social proof and human nature, it absolutely will.

People can only be expected to make the best decisions with the information that is readily available for them.

Let's dive into the types of social proof you can leverage online to continue to elevate authority, credibility, and trust.

Displaying Your Social Proof

Here are some of the different ways you can display social proof to increase trust with potential prospects:

1. Testimonials

The most important form of social proof is testimonials from your clients. These should be displayed on your website. Research done by Nielsen shows that 92 percent of people will trust a recommendation from a peer, and 70 percent of people will trust a recommendation from someone they don't even know.[19]

This includes both written and video testimonials. When sharing written testimonials, including more information about the writer is better, and this is further enhanced if you add a photo of the person providing the testimonial. While a written testimonial will always have value, include video testimonials where possible, because they're proven to be increasingly compelling. There is plenty of science to back up the power of video, which does a better job inspiring trust then capturing (and keeping) the attention of your prospects.

2. Case Studies

A well-written case study that succinctly shares the story of your customer's journey and subsequent success using your product or service is a fantastic form of social proof. Focus on the journey and how it led to the final results.

According to psychologists, Christopher Chabris and Daniel Simons, stories are persuasive and more trustworthy than statistics because individual examples stick in our minds, but statistics do not. Essentially, the story of their journey allows customers with similar challenges to imagine your product or service creating the same kind of results for them.

Another benefit is that while case studies are often written in a longer, more formal style, they are based on the idea that customers view lengthy, in-depth reviews as being more reputable than brief excerpts. They are considered to provide high authority, social proof.

3. LinkedIn Recommendations

Ask the satisfied customers who have previously provided you with a testimonial if they'd also be willing to share their testimonial in the form of a LinkedIn recommendation. Recommendations given by clients (and additional colleagues and coworkers) and displayed on LinkedIn can have great weight with potential prospects, particularly when those recommendations include details of your expertise and how you were able to help your clients.

The advantage of LinkedIn recommendations over testimonials on your website is that there is a clickable link to the profile of the person who recommended you. This validates that the recommendation is from a real person, where we know that some websites often include fake testimonials.

4. Rich Media

You can highlight client testimonials by using rich media and have them embedded right into your LinkedIn profile. Examples of rich media include video testimonials from clients and a SlideShare presentation displaying each of your client testimonials on individual slides. You can even create a PDF document, nicely designed and displaying all of your testimonials, and upload it to the rich media sections of your profile, either under your summary section or experience section.

5. Social Reach

Your social reach includes how many other people are following you on LinkedIn and other social media platforms. The quality of your content has a direct correlation to the size of your social reach. The better your content, the more people will follow you so they don't miss the new content you share. Your social reach can also be identified through the amount of engagement you get (in the form of likes, comments, and shares) on the content you post.

One of the fastest ways to damage your credibility and destroy trust is to engage in any unethical marketing practices.

Ethical Marketing

By now you're aware that relationship-building and establishing credibility and trust is essential if you want to successfully sell your product or service through social selling tactics on LinkedIn or anywhere else online.

This is why ethical considerations and character traits (honesty in particular) matter in marketing. The only way you can establish yourself as a credible and trustworthy authority to potential prospects is to exemplify those values, especially in the way you market yourself, your brand, and your products or services. And doing that is what constitutes ethical marketing.

Unfortunately, the pressure of making that all-important sale or getting attention in the noisy online world may sometimes steer some in the direction of marketing practices that are… questionable, to put it mildly. And it is at this point where your marketing becomes unethical.

Ethical vs. Unethical Marketing Tactics

The unethical marketer uses deceptive tactics and half-truths to achieve their objectives, and while they may not see the harmful effects of applying such practices in the short term, the repercussions of these actions will undoubtedly be felt by the marketer at some point.

Here are some all too common marketing practices that would be considered unethical.

Creating False Scarcity to Bolster Sales

Simply put, this happens when you create the impression that you are selling a limited-edition product (either available for a short period or only in limited quantities) just to drive your sales when there's more than enough for your customers (and, thus, no need to rush).

For example, when it comes to digital products, how in the world do you run out of copies of a digital eBook? I understand including some bonuses that are available only for a limited time to get people to take action; that's not unethical. However, to act as though a digital eBook will be completely gone in two weeks is complete nonsense.

Now imagine how your customers will feel when they inevitably learn of this deception and how this will affect their choices in the future.

Advertising "Live" Webinars That Aren't Live

Picture this scenario: One day, you receive an email from a popular marketing expert, inviting you to a "live" webinar that discusses a topic that's relevant to your industry. Because this person is an authority figure, you decide that you don't want to miss out on this opportunity.

Take note that there's emphasis on the word "live," making this a can't-miss event. According to the email, it won't even be recorded, which means that if you don't attend, you'll have to wait for the next one, if it ever happens.

The day of the webinar comes, and you're logged on with a considerable number of participants, according to the webinar platform. The webinar goes on for about an hour until you are directed to a landing page that shows the marketer's latest offer. But what if the next day, out of curiosity you click the invitation link again at the given time? To your shock and irritation, you discover that you are now tuning in to the same webinar you attended yesterday.

Don't get me wrong, I don't have an issue with recorded webinars or "evergreen webinars," but it is not necessary to lie and say it's a live event that will never be available again.

When people catch wind of the deception, this will eliminate any trust that had previously been formed. And because you were dishonest about the webinar being live, all the hard work you did to gain trust will quickly go down the drain, despite the valuable information you shared during your webinar.

Fake Testimonials

It's normal for a business to want to only display positive reviews and testimonials on their website and social profiles. However, do not ever resort to falsifying testimonials to look credible; it will damage your credibility instead.

How do you spot a fake testimonial?

It's easy; it looks something like this: Barb M. or Steve T. When a testimonial is missing a surname, you can guarantee it is FAKE. When it comes to testimonials, more information is always better.

This is what a proper testimonial looks like (notice it includes a first name, surname, title, and a location):

> *"The LinkedIn Domination system Melonie created for me allowed me to fill my sales pipeline from zero to $1.45 million in only seven months. The system works!"*
>
> ~Lori Carr, Customer Experience Consultant,
> West Palm Beach, Florida

It is better to have no testimonials than to use fake testimonials.

Incorporating a Fabricated "Lavish" Lifestyle or a Fake "Hero" Story

This covers two separate items, but both involve wealth, and they have the same objective, which is to deceive your customer into thinking that following your example (buying your product or service) will make them rich and successful.

You have seen the pictures of "experts" inside a private plane, a luxury house, a top-of-the-line car, or fancy vacation spot. While these photos are undoubtedly great for beautifying their social media profiles, the real message here is what isn't said by words. These carefully constructed images only serve to portray a certain lifestyle—more often than not, a false one—and to send a subliminal message to consumers, *"You can be me, too, by doing as I say."*

Others rely on a made up "hero story" to add credibility to the supposed effectiveness of their offered services. Have all speakers and marketers lived in the back of their car and been homeless? While it is good to incorporate brand storytelling into your marketing strategy, it certainly doesn't mean making up stories to make you appear a certain way to your audience.

Ethical Digital Marketing Tactics

So, what are some ethical marketing guidelines that you can follow?

While the answer may vary depending on who you ask, since they are based on values, I'd like to believe that some values hold true, no matter the situation or location. Here are my top four ethical marketing values:

1. **Transparency**: Don't try to pull the wool over your customers' eyes. Do not withhold truthful information that is valuable to their decision-making.

2. **Responsibility**: Make sure that you review everything you publish. Take full responsibility for the marketing materials that promote your business or brand, and make sure that you approve of them before they go up online.

3. **Fairness**: Don't stoop to low levels just to get ahead of the competition. Avoid instigating attacks or false comparisons against your competitors. The only person that looks bad when you attack a competitor is you.

4. **Honesty**: This one is perhaps the most straightforward of all: Don't lie. Remember that one small lie will lead to more (significant) lies and that it only takes one lie brought to light for your credibility to fall apart in front of your customers.

The next time you're tempted to use digital marketing tactics that go against the principles of ethical marketing, ask yourself, *"Even if this works out for me this one time, am I willing to risk my credibility, respect, and trustworthiness, just for a temporary advantage?"* Your customers—your business—should mean more to you than that.

Once trust is broken, it's almost impossible to earn back. And remember, the most significant payoff for ethical marketing, or as I like to call it, **trust-based marketing**, is that people do business with those they know, like, and trust.

Building Trust Online

As I have discussed throughout the book, one of the most important ways you can build authority, credibility, and trust is to consistently deliver value to your prospects. This means that you provide the best and most complete answers to their most significant challenges in the formats they prefer to consume. Through this process, you go well beyond merely selling a product or service but establish yourself as an authority on your topic. This is key to differentiating yourself from your competitors and becoming the number one option in the minds of your prospects.

In one study, Forrester found that 74 percent of buyers choose the company that was first to provide value as they were defining their buying vision. This makes it very clear that to increase your success and sales, you not only offer significant value to your prospects, but you also get your content in front of them—before your competition does.

By becoming part of the conversation early in the buyer's journey, you allow your target audience to get to know and trust you, therefore building the relationship. This means that when they are ready to buy, if you have created a relationship of trust and shown that you understand and can help them solve their challenge, they will come to you.

> *"Compared to economic considerations, such as price or the return on investment, trust comes out as the most important factor when closing the deal."*
>
> (Source: The State of Sales 2017)

This will never change; people always want to do business with those they trust.

Share Your Knowledge

To be truly successful at building authority, credibility, and trust, you must be willing to share your knowledge with your ideal clients and community. Not just some of it—but all of it. Your very best tips and strategies, the knowledge that makes you an expert at what you do.

Now you might be thinking, *"If I give it all away, then what do I have left to sell?"*

The answer is **you and your product or service**.

There will always be do-it-yourself types who either lack the funds to pay for your services or like the challenge of doing it themselves. They would never have paid for your services either way. But, they will share your content, and just how generous and knowledgeable you are, with their network. Then there are those who either lack the time or the desire to do what you do and will gladly pay for the services of an expert. By giving away your best information, you position yourself as a trusted authority and will be top of mind when someone is interested in what you offer.

In case you still doubt the power of generously sharing your knowledge with your ideal clients, I want to share a story about a friend of mine who was able to capture the hearts of an entire industry.

He Captured the Hearts of an Entire Industry

With his first baby due to arrive soon, Antonio Calero's panic was intense when he lost his job three weeks before the due date. He hadn't worked at his current job long enough to receive a severance package that would provide his family with a financial safety net, and his savings were minimal. Although he found a temporary job that would meet his financial needs, he longed to be able to find a job he loved.

As it happened, earlier that year, he had launched his own blog with the primary goal of sharing his digital marketing knowledge with others. Despite having found another job, Antonio found he was hooked on blogging. He loved the feeling of helping others with his knowledge, so he kept blogging, creating most of his articles in between diaper changes.

Antonio's Challenge

While Antonio was an excellent verbal communicator, he was not a natural writer. Each article he produced was hard work, and he couldn't afford a copywriter or an editor to check his grammar.

As he couldn't publish the same volume of content as other top bloggers, he committed to focusing on the quality of his content rather than quantity. When he chose a topic, he would do extensive research and add as much detail as possible. Antonio wanted to provide his few readers with the best content he could create.

The Solution

That dedication to generously giving his community his best knowledge helped him begin his journey in building authority, credibility, and trust.

Some months later, he approached a few prominent blogs, asking for an opportunity to write a guest article. One of those blogs was my blog, Top Dog Social Media. He had been expecting a straight, *"NO,"* as his blog was still tiny and didn't have much content. He was pleasantly surprised when he received an email from my team, confirming we'd be delighted to have him publish an article on our blog.

Not only did his first guest blog post help further his career, but it also put his name in front of other digital marketing influencers.

Antonio was just getting started.

You see, he had been doing something vital from the beginning—networking.

This is what Antonio said when I asked him his definition of networking, *"Networking isn't knowing a bunch of other people; it's about creating meaningful connections with people so they recognize and remember you."*

What Antonio did was build meaningful relationships.

Antonio made an effort to read and comment on every great article he read, not to get attention, but because he wanted to engage with the authors of what he considered to be exceptional content. Antonio's goal was to sincerely engage in a real conversation with other people he admired and who were interested in the same things he was. Some of the authors replied, while others were less responsive, but this did get him on the radar of many of those influencers.

The Results

Ian Clearly from RazorSocial asked Antonio to guest blog for him. This opportunity produced two significant results. First, he developed a great online friendship. Second, the article he wrote for Ian opened the door that led to where he is currently. The article was a review comparing four tools for running Facebook ads, one of which was AdEspresso. AdEspresso's CEO Massimo Chieruzzi found the article and, after commenting on it (another example of authentic and genuine networking), contacted Antonio on Twitter. It was just a friendly conversation, but Antonio was on their radar.

He went on to write guest blog posts for other websites and was continuing to elevate his authority and credibility. It was then that he took a leap of faith and asked to guest post for Social Media Examiner, where he was accepted (a big win for anyone in digital marketing).

Over the years, he also developed a relationship with Emeric Ernoult (CEO of Agorapulse), who became a friend and mentor. After Antonio published his first guest post on Social Media Examiner, he asked Emeric how he could take it to the next level. Emeric's response was clear: he needed to meet all these people in person. Exactly what I've been sharing throughout this book: to build relationships, you need to move the conversation offline.

Following his advice, Antonio went to San Diego to attend Social Media Marketing. There, Antonio found that meeting people face-to-face allowed him to accomplish much more than he could with hundreds of hours of online connection. He was able to meet some of his long time, online connections including me and the team at Social Media Examiner. He left San Diego with a lot of new connections, relationships, and business opportunities.

Then, the opportunity of a lifetime knocked on his door: Armando Biondi, AdEspresso's COO, asked Antonio if he wanted to join their company. At that moment, all of the time and effort that Antonio had invested in building authority, credibility, and trust paid off. He landed his dream job.

Takeaways

Antonio shared his key takeaways:

- Never stop following your passion. There may be times when doing what you like is hard, but don't let that stop you from chasing the opportunity to do what you love.

- While Content is King, quality is more important than quantity. Whatever you decide to do, always focus on doing an excellent job.

- Do something because you like doing it, not to gain attention or money. Your first goal is to be happy about what you do, because if you aren't happy, it's hard to make others happy.

- Networking is key. (I'd re-phrase that to relationship-building, which I know is what Antonio means by the term networking.)

- Always show your authentic personality, and follow your core values.

- When success arrives, you need to be even more authentic, humble, and passionate about what you do.

- Whenever possible, turn online relationships into offline relationships; it's offline where the magic happens.

In addition to creating high-quality content, follow the additional tips and strategies laid out in this chapter to continue to elevate your authority and credibility, and build trust.

CHAPTER NINE

ASSEMBLE YOUR SOCIAL SELLING PLAYBOOK

You are now ready to start putting all that you've learned in this book into action, with a clear outline of the highest leveraging activities you can do to start generating new leads, clients, and sales from using LinkedIn. There are so many things you could do, but many of them are time-wasters and don't produce a positive ROI—return on investment OR return on impact.

To be successful at LinkedIn, you need to have a concrete plan, with a specific list of activities that you commit to doing.

If you fail to plan, you plan to fail.

It is proven that businesses grow five times faster with a written plan. But in creating a written plan, you must know what the specific social selling activities are and why they are essential. You will then take each of these activities and create your action plan (or as I refer to it, your social selling playbook) that you will commit to.

The most important activities in this action plan will consist of the five steps in The LINK Method™, which represent the highest leveraging activities you can do to grow your business quickly through the use of LinkedIn. There are also some additional activities you can do to help you build authority, credibility, and trust, as well as remain top of mind to your network filled with potential prospects.

Figure 9.01

The LINK Method ™

Copyright © TopDogSocialMedia.com

Now let's dive into the specific activities as part of your social selling playbook on LinkedIn. Some should be done daily, others weekly, and some on an as-needed basis. I will break them into sections identifying which ones are to be done daily, weekly, or when relevant.

Daily Social Selling Activities

Activity: Find Prospects

Step 1 of The LINK Method™ requires you to mine LinkedIn for potential prospects. It's important to set a target number of new prospects to reach out to every day—the amount you decide on will be dependent upon your sales and revenue goals. How many prospects you connect with will also depend on how much time you are willing to dedicate to this. Some of my clients can only commit up to 15 minutes a day, and others find that spending 30-60 minutes a day is well worth their time as it directly correlates to the number of new clients they generate.

In Chapter 5, I covered a variety of places where you can search for prospects to connect with, including LinkedIn's robust Advanced Search function.

Review any **Saved Searches**, where LinkedIn will automatically populate people who fall into the search parameters.

Narrow your search to a more targeted list by incorporating Boolean search parameters.

Activity: Send Connection Requests

In Step 2 of The LINK Method™ you have located your potential prospects, and now it's time to connect with them by sending a personalized connection request message.

To continue growing your network, connect with others you know or have recently met. They could be existing clients, industry peers, vendors, partners, alumni, referral partners, etc.

It is essential that you send your personalized connection requests right away to people you have recently met, while they still remember you and are more likely to accept your connection request.

For example, if you just attended an event or conference and you met some people you want to stay in contact with, send them a connection request as soon as you are able, mentioning in your personalized note that you enjoyed meeting them at the event. If they also happen to be a potential prospect, you can continue with Steps 3 through 5 of The LINK Method™.

Leverage Existing Client Relationships

Your current client list provides an excellent place to start expanding your LinkedIn network. Here are eight ways to get the most out of your relationships with your clients on LinkedIn:

1. Connect with your clients
2. Follow your clients' company pages
3. Engage with their posts
4. Save as a lead (if you are using Sales Navigator)
5. Connect with others in their organization

6. Pay attention to their content, and moves/updates, and look for future opportunities

7. Build concrete relationships by staying in touch with clients—think referrals and warm introductions

8. See who your clients are connected to—many could be ideal prospects for you

Activity: Send Welcome Message to New Connections

Step 3 of The LINK Method™ involves sending a welcome message to new prospects after they have accepted your connection request. Use the message you created in Chapter 6, and add additional personalization so it doesn't come across as a templated message.

You can create multiple welcome messages if you have more than one target market. The more relevant the message is to your individual prospect's business, the more likely they are to respond. Your goal is to establish rapport and start a dialogue.

Have all of your templated messages handy in a document so that you can be much more efficient with this process, but never forget to make the message as personalized and relevant as possible to the person you are sending it to.

Activity: Accept New Connection Requests

As your presence grows on LinkedIn, more people will want to connect with you. Often, your ideal prospects may send you a connection request. Review the profiles of the incoming connection requests you are receiving. If they fall into the category of potential prospects, follow through with Steps 3 through 5 of The LINK Method™, starting with sending your welcome message.

Activity: Send Relationship-Building Messages

In Step 4 of The LINK Method™, you send a relationship-building message that is designed to continue building rapport and also to provide value to your new connection. Use the message you created in Chapter 6 and add additional personalization to it to increase the effectiveness. Make sure that any content resource you send to your potential prospect in this message is 100 percent relevant to them.

Keep track of where each connection is in The LINK Method™ message sequence. If you are using Sales Navigator, there's a convenient Tags and Notes feature. If you are using a free or Premium LinkedIn account, you need to find another method—CRM system or a third-party tool—for tracking and staying organized on when to send the next message in the sequence. In Chapter 11, I will cover more about LinkedIn Membership Levels and how to track this process in Sales Navigator.

If a dialogue begins between you and your prospect before the next message in the sequence, refer back to that conversation and edit the next message you send appropriately. Fortunately, LinkedIn makes it easy to keep track of your conversations with your connections by scrolling through the message stream for that connection. Always double check that you haven't had any other contact with them before sending the next message in your sequence.

Activity: Send Message to Move Conversation Offline

Once you have sent your relationship-building message in Step 4 of The LINK Method™, move to Step 5, which is the last message in the sequence. Here, request to move the conversation offline.

If your prospect responds positively to this message, you will move right into scheduling that offline conversation. Those prospects who respond negatively need to be removed from your list of potential prospects. Those who don't respond at all will need to be nurtured more over time. Not everyone you consider a prospect is an "ideal prospect," while others may just not be ready at this point.

Consider the following possibilities:

- They may not be an ideal prospect
- They don't need what you offer right now
- They are not currently in a position to invest in your solution
- They have other things going on (personally or professionally) that are taking a priority right now
- They need more time for you to display authority, credibility, and to trust you more
- Your messages need to be revised as they are not resonating or creating enough interest

Activity: Respond to Replies/Messages Received

Responding to messages must be done daily. It is through these conversations that you will build relationships and get to know your prospect.

While LinkedIn's message area resembles other instant messaging platforms like Facebook Messenger rather than email, it would be a mistake to treat it the same way. While you can be less formal with the people you know well, you will be communicating with potential prospects you don't know. Ensure your response is professional and well-written.

Activity: Review Who's Viewed Your Profile

When people view your profile, it presents an opportunity for you to connect with them. As I mentioned in the LinkedIn etiquette section, I do not advise starting your connection request by saying, *"I saw you viewed my profile."* However, you can indeed reach out to those people by using one of your personalized connection request messages.

These individuals have already shown some interest in your profile. If they are a potential prospect or someone else you may want to be connected to, go ahead and send them a connection request.

With a free account, you'll only see the last five people who viewed your profile, but if you have a paid account, you'll see every person who's viewed your profile in the previous 90 days.

When you are just getting started with using LinkedIn for social selling, and until you have an extensive network, you might find five or fewer people viewing your profile a day. But as you improve your profile and build your network, that number will continuously increase. At that point, you might consider upgrading your LinkedIn membership plan so that you can see everybody who has viewed your profile.

Activity: Post Status Updates

If you are serious about generating leads on LinkedIn and positioning yourself as an authority, post at least one daily status update. Most days, I will post one status update. But some days, when I come across a compelling piece of content, or I have a thought-provoking idea or tip I want to share, I post two or more times. Your connections will see your update in their newsfeed. If you are posting valuable content and insightful ideas, you will become top of mind to your network over time and enhance your authority and credibility.

SCHEDULING PRO TIP

You can't always be on LinkedIn, and there are tools available, so you don't have to be. You can pre-schedule status updates, monitor engagement and have a quick and easy place to see and respond to comments. Some social media management tools you may want to look at for scheduling posts include:

- Agorapulse
- Buffer
- Hootsuite

NOTE: You cannot schedule engagement. Engagement is meant to be a two-way-conversation and cannot be scheduled.

Make sure you are sharing valuable content that's of specific interest and value to your ideal prospects. The types of content you post could include how-to's, thoughts, insights, stories, tips, etc. The content could come in a variety of formats including:

- Text only
- Video
- Image
- Link

If you have your own blog, post a LinkedIn update sharing the link and a relevant comment every time you post to your blog. You can also share updates when you find interesting content from others, which I covered in detail in Chapter 7 on content marketing.

Activity: Review Your Notifications

Every day you should review your Notifications to look for engagement opportunities. This will show you all the people who have engaged with your content, have followed you, have liked your updates, or have taken any other action that involves you on LinkedIn. You can then look for an opportunity to connect with them, reply to their comments, or begin a private conversation with them.

Figure 9.02

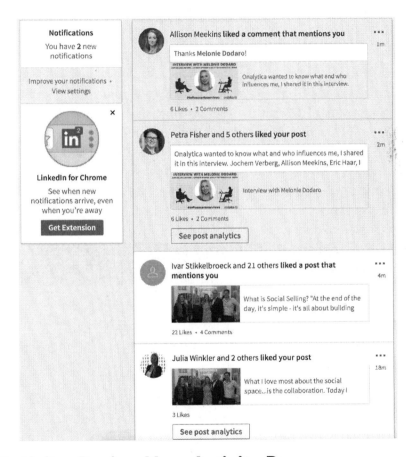

Activity: Review Your Activity Page

Engagement is an essential part of building relationships and generating new clients. When one of your connections takes the time to read and engage with your content, it is crucial that you respond to acknowledge them.

This engagement also presents an opportunity for you to build a relationship with your connections. When a connection, who is also a prospect or client, likes, comments, or shares your update or post, this is a great chance to thank them and start a conversation.

Review the engagement that you get from your updates and posts, and look for these opportunities to reply and, when relevant, start a dialogue. You can see who has interacted with your status updates and LinkedIn Publisher posts on your Activity page.

Status updates and Publisher posts can help you get seen by your 2nd-degree connections and beyond when your 1st-degree connections begin to engage with your posts. When your 1st-degree connections like or comment on your status updates, your 2nd-degree connections will see your content and have the opportunity to engage with it as well. When you see 2nd- and 3rd-degree connections engage with your content (likes, comments, or shares), this trigger event provides you the opportunity to connect and engage with them on LinkedIn. I discussed trigger events to pay attention to in Chapter 6.

CONNECTION PRO TIP

It is a great time to reach out and send a connection request when a 2nd- or 3rd-degree connection engages positively with your content. Here is an example connection request you can use when this occurs:

Hey <Name>,

I noticed that you <liked/commented/shared> the article I posted on <topic>. Thought it would be great to connect here on LinkedIn and share ideas.

<Your Name>

That wraps up the daily activities that are a necessary part of your social selling playbook. Now let's cover the activities to do on a weekly basis.

Weekly Social Selling Activities

Activity: Nurture Prospects (Focus on Hot Prospects)

Prospects that didn't respond to your request to move the conversation offline require further nurturing. When you come across something that would be of interest to them (article, news, stat, case study, etc.), you can send them a private message letting them know you came across something you thought they'd be interested in, so you wanted to share it with them. Using content that is not your own is often useful at this stage as it feels more genuine that you came across something that made you think of them.

Some of my past students in my online courses have used this strategy very effectively in sharing my content on LinkedIn with prospects, as many people who use LinkedIn would like to learn how to use it more effectively.

Nurturing prospects is especially crucial if you have a list of people you consider falling into the hot prospect category. Hot prospects are the people you want to stay in touch with, monitor, and continue to follow up with. After you've taken them through The LINK Method™ message sequence, you want to stay in contact without irritating them with frequent messages.

The goal is to become a resource for these hot prospects by sending them insightful and high-quality content. Again, if you find an article or something that's of value to them, send it along with a personal note as to why you thought they'd be interested in it.

PROSPECTING PRO EXERCISE

When you come across an article you want to share with a prospect, you can do it right within the article by clicking on the LinkedIn share button.

Type their name or email address in the box that pops up when you use the share button. As always, customize and personalize any of the messages you send.

For example, you might write:

Hi <Name>,
I just came across this article called <name of article>.
<Share interesting facts, stats, or info from article>.
Let me know if you have any questions about <topic> best practices,
and I'd be happy to answer them.
<Your Name>

Activity: Post Article on LinkedIn Publisher

If building authority, credibility, and trust is your goal, then creating high-value content should be a priority. In addition to posting content on your blog, you can also post content on LinkedIn Publisher.

Essentially, LinkedIn Publisher gives you your own publishing platform that is similar to a blog and can expand your reach far beyond your own personal network.

Your posts are displayed on your profile in your Activity box, shared with your first-degree connections in their homepage newsfeed, and can be distributed more broadly as they are shared.

LinkedIn Publisher posts are also indexed by Google and show up in organic search results. For example, if you Google the term "LinkedIn etiquette" you'll see an article I published years ago on LinkedIn Publisher that still ranks as the number one result for that search term at the time of this writing. What's even more interesting, this article was published first on my site, Top Dog Social Media, which is not showing up on the first page of the search results. Take advantage of the powerful Google indexing that is available by posting articles to LinkedIn Publisher.

Figure 9.03

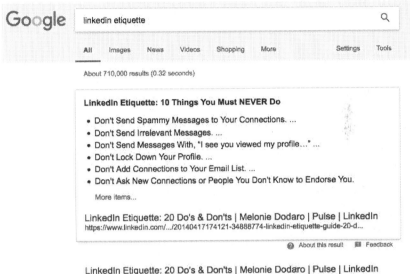

A great place to start is by re-posting the most popular and relevant articles from your blog onto LinkedIn Publisher. You can do this by cutting and pasting the text of your entire article, then adding the title, cover image, and any other graphics or media. To ensure that Google has indexed the post on your website first, wait at least a few days after posting the article on your blog to republish on Publisher.

LINKEDIN PUBLISHER PRO TIP

To increase the number of views your post gets, be sure to add a cover image. If you don't have access to a graphic designer to create one for you, you can easily create a cover image using any of the free graphics tools available such as Canva, Adobe Post or PicMonkey.

You can also embed other types of rich media to your articles including:

Images: JPG, GIF or PNG
Videos: YouTube, SlideShare, TED, Getty, Vimeo and more
Slides: SlideShare, Prezi, inVision and more

Activity: Request Warm Introductions and Referrals

A great way to build your network and jumpstart potential relationships with new connections is by having a mutual connection introduce you. This is known as a warm introduction.

Each week, you should look at your 2nd-degree connections for potential prospects that you would like to connect with and then see who you are mutually connected to, and request a warm introduction from those you know well enough to ask.

Look for opportunities for an introduction and leverage your 1st-degree connection as a conversation starter. This could take the form of asking your connection the question, *"I see we're both connected to <Name of 2nd-degree connection>. Do you know them personally, or are you just connected on LinkedIn?"* If they say they know them personally, then politely ask for a warm introduction. This is explained in more detail in Chapter 6.

Additional Social Selling Playbook Activities

Activity: Give and Request Recommendations

You know the old saying, givers get?

I suggest you provide a recommendation to someone in your network whenever an appropriate opportunity presents itself. If there's somebody in your network who you feel comfortable recommending and whose credibility and expertise you can vouch for, then go ahead and write them a recommendation. When that person accepts your recommendation on their profile, LinkedIn prompts them to return the favor and recommend you. The law of reciprocity in action.

Not everybody will do so. In fact, not everybody should. For example, many people recommend me because they've attended one of my speaking engagements or participated in one of my webinars or online courses, but I don't know them personally. So if they provide me with a recommendation, I can't return the favor because I don't know them or their work.

When appropriate, ask individuals that have worked with you for a recommendation. I strongly suggest following the formula I shared with you in an earlier chapter to do this successfully.

Activity: Endorse Others' Skills

In your notifications, you will see when people have endorsed you for your skills. Likewise, they will see you in their notifications when you have endorsed them. When appropriate, why not endorse someone in your network? This is a popular feature of LinkedIn because it's so simple. You click the little "+" icon beside the skill listed that you want to endorse someone for.

Unfortunately, too many people are endorsing random people they don't know, which can undermine the value of endorsements. There is, however, a level of social proof here whether people realize it or not. When you see a profile of a person who has lots of endorsements, people assume that that person is proficient in that particular skill.

What is even more important is that those endorsements may help you move higher up in the search results for those specific skills (keywords). If you get 100 endorsements for a particular keyword and somebody else has only 10 endorsements for the same keyword, you could potentially show up higher in the search results when someone is searching for that keyword.

Another benefit to endorsing others is when they receive a notification that you've endorsed them; this could result in a conversation or them reciprocating and endorsing some of your skills.

There you have it, all the activities that will be used in your social selling playbook to begin generating more leads and clients for your business. Are you ready to put them into action?

CHAPTER TEN

THE MONEY IS IN THE EXECUTION

Now that I have laid out the specific and highest leveraging activities that form part of your social selling playbook, it is time to put it all together to create a written plan you can follow daily and weekly.

This playbook is necessary to help you turn your lead generation goals into reality. A lack of clarity is responsible for a lack of action. At this point, you should have complete clarity on precisely what you need to do and how often. By having this written plan, you're going to persevere and be more effective and efficient and ultimately produce a steady stream of new clients for your business.

Documenting Your Social Selling Playbook

"Setting a goal is not the main thing. It is deciding how you will go about achieving it and staying with that plan."

-Tom Landry

The first thing you need to determine is how many prospects you want to connect with each day. Next, decide how much time you can devote to your action plan every day, whether it is 15 minutes, 30 minutes, or 60 minutes or more. Whatever it is, be consistent because the more consistent you are, the better your results will be.

Now you need to turn your list of activities into a written social selling playbook.

- Start by creating a document that itemizes the activities that were recommended and listed in Chapter 9

- Now itemize the activities by how often you will do them, in chronological order (first daily, then weekly, then as-needed)

- List each of the activities in the order of importance with the most critical tasks at the top

PRINT IT OUT. You did not create this to be another lost document on your computer that never gets used. Use it every day. Check off each activity as you complete it.

Sample Social Selling Playbook

Here is a sample social selling playbook that lists out the specific activities that you can and should be doing. Use this as a guideline to create one that will work for you.

Sample Social Selling Playbook

Daily

Find prospects

Send connection requests to potential prospects (10 daily)

Send connection requests to people you know or have just met

Send welcome messages to new connections

Accept new connection requests

Send relationship-building messages
Send a message to move conversation offline
Respond to replies/messages received
Review who's viewed your profile
Post status update
Review notifications
Review activity page
Weekly
Nurture prospects (focus on hot prospects)
Post article on LinkedIn Publisher
Request warm introductions
When Appropriate
Give and request recommendations
Endorse other's skills

Your Social Selling Playbook

Your social selling playbook needs to work for you and your schedule. You must decide based on your schedule or time availability. You may also want to bulk some of the daily tasks and do them less often. For example, instead of finding prospects and sending connection requests to 10 new ones daily, you may want to do it once a week and send 50 out in one day.

Also, instead of posting a daily status update, you can preschedule them a week at a time. Any way you choose to execute your social selling playbook is fine as long as you are consistent and as long as you don't neglect engagement and miss potential opportunities.

Be sure also to create a content marketing checklist that includes the days you will dedicate to creating, editing, and publishing content as well as when and where you will share it, etc.

Remember, the key is consistency!

Now it's time to get even more specific and create a social selling playbook you are prepared to stick with. Remember that money is in the execution of this playbook, and your results will be a direct reflection of the effort you put into implementing it.

Social Selling Playbook

Monday

Tuesday

Wednesday

Thursday

Friday

Next, have a documented schedule for your content marketing activities. Get specific and be realistic in what you are prepared to commit to.

Content Marketing Checklist

Monday

Tuesday

Wednesday

Thursday

Friday

Executing Your Social Selling Playbook

The more specific you are with the activities and days you will do them, the more likely it is you will be executing it. You must be committed to following your playbook.

Review your playbook as needed to adjust anything that's not working for you. If on Tuesdays you are usually tied up with clients all day, you may only have time to check into LinkedIn to respond to messages you've received and respond to comments people have made on your posts.

You should review your playbook quarterly (or more often if needed) to see if you need to increase the number of prospects you are connecting with to meet and exceed your revenue goals. If your messages, or content, are not getting the response you want, you may need to adjust your strategy or hire someone to help you refine it.

As you become more familiar and comfortable with this process, you may also find new ways of improving the efficiency of your social selling playbook and content marketing plan.

The key is to create a system and a routine that become second nature, to utilize this powerful social selling tool to maximize your results in generating new prospects and clients. I urge you to implement everything you have learned in this book—creating a compelling profile and personal brand, implementing The LINK Method™, sharing great content, increasing your authority, growing your network, targeting specific prospects, and staying organized. If you do this consistently, you will have a steady and predictable stream of new prospects and clients to keep your sales pipeline full at all times.

SOCIAL SELLING PRO TIP

To improve the efficiency of your content marketing and social selling playbook as you go through the various activities, make a quick note of how long each action takes you. You might want to do this for a couple of weeks, especially if you are just starting. This will help you plan and manage your time and activities better.

You will find that as you become more competent and confident in executing your social selling playbook, many of the activities will take less time. Test what works for you and what isn't working, and modify your strategy and plan when needed.

Then test them again. I can't stress the importance of testing to help you improve what you are doing, by finding out what is or isn't working.

Have patience! It takes a while to build a LinkedIn network extensive enough to generate a substantial amount of search results for your target market. However, if you are interested in achieving those results faster, it is indeed possible to do by increasing your time and effort and considering the investment of upgrading your LinkedIn membership to Sales Navigator (which I will discuss in the next chapter).

Measure What Matters: Key Performance Indicators

KPIs are merely the results or outcomes that you want to achieve from your social selling efforts. If you are going to put in consistent time and energy every day, then I am confident you want to accomplish some definable and measurable results. Your ultimate success requires that you can answer these two fundamental questions:

1. What are the outcomes I want from the social selling efforts?

2. Do I have access to data that support those outcomes to measure success?

While there are many social selling KPIs that can be tracked and measured, here are a few that will provide you with some insights into both the activities you are doing as well as the results from doing them.

Remember: *You can't improve what you don't measure.*

Social Selling Metrics to Track

There's a wide range of social selling metrics you should be tracking, they include:

- Number of leads from social selling
- Number of offline conversations generated
- Value of sales pipeline from social selling
- Contract value of deals made from social selling
- Revenue generated from social selling activities

Additional metrics that are not revenue focused but worth tracking as they share insights into the activities you are doing, include:

- Number of views from posts or shared content
- Engagement with shared content (likes, comments, shares, etc.)
- Visits to your website that come from LinkedIn
- Network size (connections, followers)

Figure 10.01

If there are any additional KPIs that are important to you, include them in the list you want to track and measure.

Now create a list of the KPIs you want to track and measure.

KPI's	Start	Month One	Month Two	Month Three

There's no better time than now to start implementing your social selling playbook. Continuously track your efforts to perfect your strategy and process so that it is delivering specific and tangible results week after week.

Download the **FREE companion workbook** that includes all of these templates (social selling playbook, content marketing checklist, and KPIs): **http://LinkedInUnlockedWorkbook.com**

Now let's cover the different membership levels LinkedIn offers so you can decide which one is right for you.

CHAPTER ELEVEN

LINKEDIN MEMBERSHIP: FREE VS. PREMIUM VS. SALES NAVIGATOR

In this chapter, I will outline the differences in the levels of LinkedIn membership: Free, Premium Business Plus, and Sales Navigator Professional. Also, I will go into greater detail on the functionality of Sales Navigator for those who are serious about using LinkedIn as a tool to generate new leads and clients on a consistent basis.

I have put together a breakdown of the usefulness of each LinkedIn membership level compared to its cost and how they can be of benefit to you.

Free LinkedIn Membership

With continuous changes to the free membership and removal of once-free features and tools, many are left wondering if LinkedIn is still useful with a free account or if they need some level of a paid account for it to be a worthwhile investment of their time and resources.

Even with what has been lost, LinkedIn is still the best place for professionals, B2B businesses, marketers, and salespeople to find and connect with their ideal clients.

With a free account, you can still find and connect with your ideal clients, post regular status updates and LinkedIn Publisher posts, as well as engage in numerous ways with your connections.

What is missing from a free account is the ability to tag people and stay organized with your social selling efforts. However, I'll also mention in this chapter a lower cost third-party tool that can allow you to tag people and make notes. Please note, I do not financially or otherwise benefit from any tool that I recommend, and I am providing completely objective information.

One of the other challenges with a free account is that if you want to do a lot of searches for prospects, you will face the commercial search limits LinkedIn imposes on free accounts. This will present a challenge for those who want to be very active in prospecting on LinkedIn.

Commercial Use Limit (Straight from LinkedIn)

If you reach the commercial use limit, your activity on LinkedIn indicates that you're likely using it for commercial use, like hiring or prospecting. This limit is calculated based on your search activity since the first day of the calendar month.

Specific activities that contribute to the limit include:

- Searching for LinkedIn profiles on LinkedIn.com and mobile
- Browsing LinkedIn profiles using the People Also Viewed section located on the right side of a profile

These activities do not count toward the limit:

- Searching profiles by name using the search box located at the top of every page on LinkedIn.com
- Browsing your 1st-degree connections from the connections page
- Searching for jobs on the jobs page

You'll see a warning as you approach the limit. Your free monthly usage resets at midnight PST on the first day of each calendar month. The exact number of searches or views you have left will not be displayed, and LinkedIn cannot lift the limit upon request. Also, note that the warning that you are approaching the limit may not display if you run through the full number of searches or views too quickly.

To avoid the commercial search limit, you need to upgrade to one of LinkedIn's Premium account plans to increase the number of profile searches and views you have available. These account plans are:

- Premium Business

- Recruiter

- Sales Navigator

Premium Business Plus Membership

It can be hard to know which paid plan will work best for you.

If you are like many people, considering a paid LinkedIn account may be necessary to achieve the results you are looking for. Look at the factors that are relevant to your business such as the value of your average sale, the time and resources you have available, and your budget.

To avoid the commercial search limit, you need to have at least a Premium Business Plus plan. However, the Premium plan is an incredibly pared down version of Sales Navigator. When you look at the features and tools you get with each plan compared to the pricing difference, the small extra investment to move up to Sales Navigator will make it the better investment for most individuals and businesses.

If you are still unsure about how useful the tools and benefits of the paid plans are for your social selling efforts, there are free trials available for both plan levels. I would recommend choosing the trial for Sales Navigator as you will get the chance to experience and experiment with all of the features and tools available.

Here is a quick overview of the comparison between different plans provided by LinkedIn.

Figure 11.01

FEATURES		LINKEDIN FREE	PREMIUM BUSINESS	SALES NAVIGATOR PROFESSIONAL	SALES NAVIGATOR TEAM	SALES NAVIGATOR ENTERPRISE
See when prospects check you out	Who's Viewed My Profile	Last 5 people	Last 90 days	Last 90 days	Last 90 days	Last 90 days
Reach prospects directly	InMails (per month)	·	15	20	30	50
	PointDrive presentations (per month)	·	·	·	10	Unlimited
Find the right leads and accounts	Extended LinkedIn Network Access	·	√	√	√	√
	Advanced Sales-Specific Search Tools	·	·	√	√	√
	Saved Leads	·	·	1,500	5,000	10,000
	Automatic Lead & Account Recommendations	·	·	√	√	√
	Territory Preferences	·	·	√	√	√
Stay organized and up-to-date on leads & accounts you're interested in	Job Change Alerts	·	·	√	√	√
	Prospect & Company News Alerts	·	·	√	√	√
	Notes & Tags	·	·	√	√	√
	Sales Navigator for Gmail	·	·	√	√	√
Training and education	Sales Navigator Learning Center	·	·	√	√	√
Leverage LinkedIn wherever you work	Dedicated Mobile App	·	·	√	√	√
	CRM Widgets	·	·	·	√	√
	CRM Sync (with Write-Back)	·	·	·	√	√
Access the entire LinkedIn network	Out-of-Network Unlocks (per month)	·	·	·	25	25
Unlock the power of your company's social graph	Warm Introductions through TeamLink	·	·	·	Team network	Company network
Enterprise Capabilities	Seat Management	·	·	·	Basic	Enterprise-grade
	Usage Reporting	·	·	·	√	√
	Single-Sign-On Integration	·	·	·	·	√
Billing and Support	Volume and Multi-Year Discounts	·	·	·	√	√
	Invoicing	·	·	·	√	√
	Dedicated Relationship Manager	·	·	·	√	√
				Start your free trial	Request free demo	Request free demo

When you are actively using LinkedIn for social selling to generate new leads, managing what messages you have sent to whom can become confusing. It can be taxing to try to remember to whom you have sent a connection request, which of those requests were accepted, what message you may have sent last to a lead, and when you sent that message.

This is why it is so vital that you have a tool or system in place to help keep you organized and on top of your social selling activities.

The Business Case for Sales Navigator

If you are serious about generating leads on LinkedIn and will be actively following the social selling activities I have laid out throughout this book, you need a robust tool that will not only help you stay organized but will also make it quicker and easier for you to find and communicate with your leads, prospects, and clients.

This is precisely what LinkedIn Sales Navigator will help you do. With the many social selling tools that Sales Navigator includes, you will be able to create an efficient and effective process that you can fine tune as you master it and implement your social selling playbook. The most significant downside is the cost, but depending on what a sale is worth for you, it can easily be worth the investment to help you fill your sales pipeline with targeted prospects.

For example, a sales professional who uses Sales Navigator for their social selling can quickly save themselves 30 minutes a day as the process becomes more and more efficient. That adds up to around 10 hours a month. What would it be worth to you if you had 10 hours a month extra for your sales activities?

If you are not already a Sales Navigator user, you can start by signing up for the free trial, which gives you a month to decide if you want to continue using it.

If you are considering upgrading your LinkedIn membership to actively generate new leads and prospects, LinkedIn Sales Navigator Professional provides the most useful tools for the investment.

Depending on your goals and resources, you may only ever need to use the free version of LinkedIn. But there are many premium features that are available with Sales Navigator you may want to have:

- Advanced Search with extra filters
- Saved Searches (up to 15)
- Who's Viewed Your Profile (last 90 days)
- InMail
- Extended LinkedIn Network Access
- Notes and Tagging
- Automatic Lead and Account Recommendations

- Job Change Alerts
- Learning Center

Advanced Search

While the Advanced Search found within LinkedIn can be helpful to find your ideal clients, with the extensive search filters found in Sales Navigator you can precisely search for your exact ideal clients, and you can save those searches to receive new results every day, week, or month automatically. In fact, you have access to over three-dozen more filters in Sales Navigator, which will allow you to narrow your search, save you time, and create better results.

The search filters are categorized in two ways: People Search Filters (which LinkedIn calls Leads) and Company Search Filters (which LinkedIn calls Accounts).

Advanced Lead Search

- Profile filters:
  - Keywords
  - Geography
  - Relationship
  - Industry
  - Postal code
  - School
  - First name
  - Last name
  - Profile language
- Role and tenure filters
  - Function
  - Title

- ○ Seniority level
- ○ Years in current position
- ○ Years at current company
- ○ Years of experience
- Company filters
  - ○ Company
  - ○ Company headcount
  - ○ Past company
  - ○ Company type
- Other filters
  - ○ Tag
  - ○ Groups
  - ○ Member since
  - ○ Posted content keywords

Further fine-tuning can be done by applying the following criteria to your search results:

- Show only Teamlink connections
- Apply your sales preferences

Once you have your list of results, you can filter it even further by:

- Exclude saved leads
- Exclude viewed leads
- Exclude contacted leads
- Search within my accounts
- Changed jobs in the past 90 days
- Mentioned in the news in past 30 days
- Posted on LinkedIn in past 30 days
- Share experiences with you
- Leads that follow your company on LinkedIn

Advanced Account (Company) Search

- Top filters
  - Keywords
  - Geography
  - Industry
- Size filters
  - Company headcount
    - Department headcount
  - Annual revenue
  - Company headcount growth
  - Department headcount growth
  - Fortune (Fortune 50 – Fortune 1000)
- Other filters
  - Technologies used
  - Relationship
  - Job opportunities

Once you see your Account results, you can narrow your results further by only displaying Accounts with senior leadership changes in the past three months.

Figure 11.02

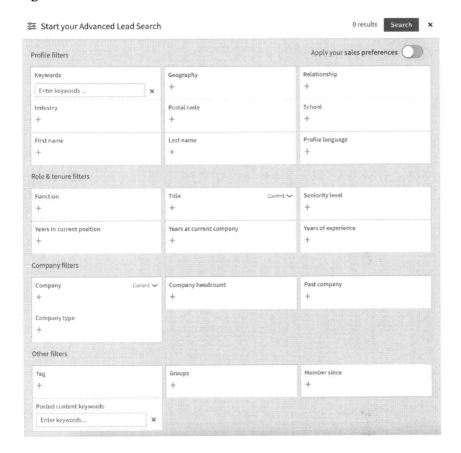

Saved Searches

After you have had the chance to modify and try different search parameters in the Advanced Search and you are satisfied with your results, you can then save your search and have LinkedIn send you daily, weekly, or monthly updates with only the new results. Sales Navigator allows you to save up to 15 saved searches versus only three with a free account; plus, you have all the additional advanced filtering, which provides much more targeted search results.

SALES NAVIGATOR PRO TIP

Create a specific search that represents your hottest group of prospects, and then fine-tune your selection to only include the people who have posted on LinkedIn in the past 30 days. LinkedIn will send you an email every day with a list of your hottest prospects who have just posted something on LinkedIn.

This provides you with a specific trigger event that allows you to engage with them on their most recent activity easily.

Using the same search criteria of your hottest prospects, create one more search adding the filter to include the people following your company. Save that search, and LinkedIn will send you a message when a hot prospect has started following your company on LinkedIn. There's hardly a better buying signal than when a prospect starts following your company.

Who's Viewed Your Profile?

An excellent source of potential connections can be found in your Who's Viewed Your Profile page. This page provides you with a list of people who have recently viewed your profile. While free members can only see the last five people who have viewed their profile, Sales Navigator members get to see the full list of people from the previous 90 days.

On top of being able to see the entire list of people who viewed your profile in the last 90 days within Sales Navigator itself, you'll get some additional insights when you view the same list within the regular LinkedIn environment. LinkedIn will show you the top companies of people visiting your profile and the most common job title. These trends can be helpful as they may identify a potential prospect or company to target. Is there some common theme or reason that these people are viewing your profile?

If you notice a trend that's outside your target market, you may want to do some discovery as to why your profile is appearing to this group.

InMail

These are messages you send directly within LinkedIn to another member with whom you are not already connected. InMail could be utilized if you want to send a message to someone before trying to connect with them via a connection request. You can also use InMail to message someone who has not yet accepted your connection request.

It is essential that when you send an InMail, you provide a valid reason for messaging them and that your message does NOT include any sales materials or pitches.

It is only possible to send InMails with a premium subscription. You are given 20 InMail credits per month with a Sales Navigator account. You can accumulate your credits from month to month, but they will expire after 90 days.

SALES NAVIGATOR PRO TIP

When sending InMails, keep these tips in mind:

- Include a compelling subject line
- Be sure to make your message about them (WIIFM) and tell them why you are messaging them—without including anything that could be perceived as a sales pitch
- Be personable, find commonality or compliment them or their profile
- Keep it short
- Include a clear call to action

Extended LinkedIn Network Access

With Extended LinkedIn Network Access, you don't have to worry about the Commercial Use Limits that apply to free accounts. This means you will not lose access to search results part way through the month, which would negatively affect your ability to do advanced searches for prospects.

No one knows exactly what number of searches you are limited to per month as a free member, but LinkedIn suggests that if you hit the limit, you are likely using the search for commercial purposes such as prospecting or lead generation. Unless your social selling goals are relatively small each month, there is a great benefit to having Extended LinkedIn Network Access.

Notes and Tags

A monthly subscription to Sales Navigator gives you the ability to add Notes and Tags to the profiles of your prospects, as well as to the companies you wish to follow. This is a crucial strategy to stay organized for anyone using LinkedIn for lead generation and social selling.

Every single time you find a prospect or when you connect with a person, you should tag them in Sales Navigator and put them in a specific tag group based on who they are. For example, are they a prospect, a strategic partner, or an existing client?

SALES NAVIGATOR PRO TIP

When you start using a lot of Tags in Sales Navigator, you may find it practical to add a # before the tags you use most often as they will then appear at the top of your list of tags.

Automatic Lead and Account Recommendations

Sales Navigator makes it easier than ever to locate potential prospects with the Suggested Leads and Suggested Accounts features that come with this account plan. Suggested Leads shows you recent updates posted by people Sales Navigator recommends based on their similarity to other leads you have recently saved and based on the sales preferences that you saved in your Sales Navigator settings. You can easily see and interact with them as well as save them.

Additionally, the Suggested Accounts feature also allows you to save a company as an Account, making it easy for you to view the company or go on to see other businesses similar to it.

Once you have tagged your prospects appropriately, you should add any relevant information about them in the notes section so that you can use that information in future interactions with them. This will allow you to stay organized and efficient and allow you to build a relationship with your prospects more effectively.

SALES NAVIGATOR PRO TIP

Sales Navigator will send you weekly emails informing you of potential trigger events with updates on *Lead shares, Company news, Company shares* and *Potential leads* based on the people and companies you have saved as leads or are following.

This information will help you make social selling much more efficient and effective.

Figure 11.03

Job Change Alerts

With the Job Change feature, Sales Navigator will notify you when one of your leads changes jobs. This can be very useful, such as when determining who you should be communicating with at a particular company, or if a prospect is now working at a company that could be a prospective new client.

The Job Change feature also presents a good reason to reach out and engage with that person, which helps to keep you top of mind. The feature makes it easy for you to see their old job and new position, as well as the ability to message them effortlessly.

Learning Center

Your monthly subscription gives you access to LinkedIn's Learning Center, which can be found in Sales Navigator and within LinkedIn itself. In the Learning Center, you will find a wide variety of courses and content under three central themes:

1. Business

2. Creative

3. Technology

You will also find many training materials available on how to use Sales Navigator. Whether you are just looking to brush up your knowledge on a particular topic or learn something new, this is an excellent resource you should make use of.

The Downside to Sales Navigator

As I mentioned previously, one downside of Sales Navigator for some may be the cost. On the other hand, if you offset that against the time this tool can save you and the value of a sale related to your activities using it, that should no longer be an argument.

A notable downside though is the development of Sales Navigator seems to be slower than the development of LinkedIn itself. Some would argue that it's inevitable as only a fraction of the total number of over half a billion LinkedIn members uses Sales Navigator.

On the other hand, these are the members who are paying a considerable amount of money to LinkedIn for a premium experience and, as such, should expect to receive a premium product that, in some aspects, is not *behind* when compared to LinkedIn itself. There are companies with over 1,000 Sales Navigator Licenses. You can do the math as to what they are paying LinkedIn each month for a user experience that's somewhat sub-par. Examples include:

- The way the LinkedIn profiles are (currently) displayed on Sales Navigator was the way they were before LinkedIn changed the user interface

- You're (currently) not able to see who else liked a post from one of your leads

- You're (currently) not able to tag people and companies when commenting on an update

One final downside is that LinkedIn with its Sales Navigator tool seems to be focusing more and more on corporate accounts, offering specific tools only to companies that sign up for eight accounts or more. From a short-term sales point of view, that may make sense for LinkedIn as there are *only* just over 20,000 companies with 10,000 employees or more. However, with the millions of independent professionals on LinkedIn, from a long-term point of view, it may not be a smart move to not specifically target this group.

Even though Sales Navigator is not perfect, seamless, or incredibly user-friendly, I still use and recommend it.

If you intend on being a professional social seller, it is worth the monthly investment.

Third-Party Tool That Provides Tagging and Notes

LinkedIn has many features and functionalities that are continually changing and adapting to the evolving needs of its user base. There are, however, tools that were made specifically to enhance LinkedIn's built-in functions. Whether your goal is to attract new prospects, create new connections in your industry, or increase the effectiveness and ROI of your social selling strategies, you will find some third-party tools that will enhance your results and your overall experience in using the LinkedIn platform.

Dux-Soup

One tool that I like is Dux-Soup. It's a strange name for a tool but is ideal for those who need more than the free LinkedIn membership but don't want to pay the full cost of Sales Navigator. Dux-Soup is an affordable and user-friendly alternative. This Chrome plug-in is ideal for those who have a limited budget or are just starting out.

Dux-Soup is a database-building tool that allows you to track the LinkedIn profiles you visit. It provides you with complete information on the profiles you visited from their contact numbers and email addresses to their company affiliations and locations.

You can opt to use the free version, which enables you to view 100 LinkedIn profiles a day, or upgrade to the paid version, which allows you to set the number of profile visits to make per day and export the CSV file. As the tool is integrated with your Chrome browser, one of the biggest benefits of using Dux-Soup is that it works right within LinkedIn, so you don't have to have multiple windows open.

Dux-Soup is a plug-in for the Chrome browser. To use it, you MUST:

- Use the Chrome browser
- Download the Dux-Soup plug-in
- Allow Dux-Soup to access your LinkedIn account

Choosing the Right LinkedIn Membership for You

Whether you decide to invest in Sales Navigator, use the free LinkedIn membership, or invest in a third-party tool, the key is to stay organized with your social selling activities.

While it may seem like a lot more work to set up your system in the beginning, not only will being organized save you time and effort in the long run, but it will prevent you from getting overwhelmed and enable you to generate leads more efficiently. You can also avoid making costly mistakes that come with being disorganized, such as sending the wrong message in the wrong context at the wrong time.

With tools like Sales Navigator, getting and staying organized is faster and easier but also provides additional tools that will help you to be even more successful with your social selling activities.

If you are interested in learning more about Sales Navigator, there are two ways. LinkedIn Learning is free with your Sales Navigator account and provides many tutorials on how to set up and effectively use Sales Navigator. Also, my friend and colleague, Perry van Beek, has written a book called *LinkedIn Sales Navigator for Dummies*; you can find it on Amazon.

CHAPTER TWELVE

THE ROI OF SOCIAL SELLING ON LINKEDIN

The digital transformation that began several years ago will continue to be a significant factor in sales and marketing going forward. Some individuals and businesses have been slow to embrace the change—or perhaps don't know where their focus should be to compete on an ever-changing playing field.

The rules of marketing are changing, and if you want to continue to bring in new clients and generate more sales, you need to change your marketing strategies as well.

Social selling works; not because it is a gimmick or a way to inundate your target market with your marketing message, but because it is built upon our human need to create trust and build relationships. It is an ongoing process; just like any relationship, it requires regular time and upkeep.

The benefit of this is, when these prospects are ready to buy, you will have positioned yourself as someone they know, like, and trust. You have set yourself up as the first choice in their minds.

Please remember that before you begin the social selling process on LinkedIn, you must ensure that *your profile is professional looking, optimized for searches,* and *speaks to your ideal clients.*

You must also make sure that you understand and follow the best practices of LinkedIn. Failure to do so could mean consequences that range from annoying potential prospects to having your LinkedIn profile restricted.

I want to share with you in a visual format what this process looks like in the Social Selling Framework through which I take my clients.

Figure 12.01

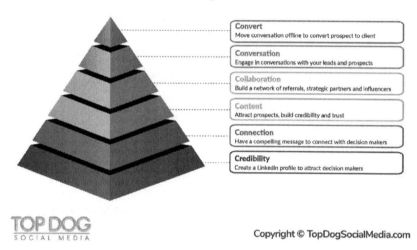

Social Selling Framework

Convert
Move conversation offline to convert prospect to client

Conversation
Engage in conversations with your leads and prospects

Collaboration
Build a network of referrals, strategic partners and influencers

Content
Attract prospects, build credibility and trust

Connection
Have a compelling message to connect with decision makers

Credibility
Create a LinkedIn profile to attract decision makers

TOP DOG
SOCIAL MEDIA

Copyright © TopDogSocialMedia.com

Following the steps laid out in this book and visually represented in the Social Selling Framework will guarantee that you receive an ROI that's worth the investment of time you put into this.

I also want to share some mistakes for you to avoid, ones that could lower your ROI.

Mistakes That Can Prevent You from Getting an ROI with Social Selling

Letting Fear Rule

Individuals and businesses are often afraid of investing in something because their past investments haven't paid off. Because strategies such as pay-per-click or SEO didn't generate significant leads, in their minds, it feels safer to avoid any risks and avoid social selling altogether.

Lacking a Structure for Content Marketing

Businesses often lack the content strategy that engages and builds trust with prospects, so they don't share, connect, and communicate. For some companies, those in sales and marketing are still working in silos. For example, marketing will create materials that cannot be used by their sales team in the social selling process.

Failing to Change Paradigms

The sales model has drastically changed over the past 10 years, with 90 percent of decision-makers not responding to cold calls. Buyers are now digitally connected, socially engaged, and using their mobile phones for almost everything. The role of sales is to build trust, and prospects must believe that you can provide the solution to their problems. In the past, ABC meant "Always Be Closing." Today, it more appropriately means "Always Be Connecting."

Failing to Build a Strong Network

Individuals and businesses fail to develop a strong network with prospects and clients. Instead, they are just accumulating connections and not building relationships—in this instance they are simply a LION (LinkedIn Open Networker). It's important to engage with and add value to connections.

Talking with the Wrong People

On social media, you can spend all day talking with people and never interact with the *right* people. Avoid this social selling mistake by clarifying who your ideal clients and prospects are and speaking to them.

Focusing on the Wrong Social Platform

Perhaps you've been spending time on other social media platforms with limited success and, until now, haven't realized the potential that LinkedIn offers in connecting you to your ideal clients. If you provide a B2B product or service, there is no better network to communicate with prospects than LinkedIn.

Not Answering *WIIFM*

The best way to alienate potential customers is to make it all about you. If you prioritize the sale over customers' pain points or desires, all of your results with social selling will fail. There's only one thing your prospect is thinking about, and that's *WIIFM* (*what's in it for me?*). Answer that question, and you'll win a lot more sales.

The ROI with Social Selling

Nearly 63 percent of sales professionals say social selling has become one of the keys to closing deals. A social selling initiative undertaken by IBM increased sales by almost 400 percent.

As far as social selling goes, there are many other impressive numbers to look at:

- According to a LinkedIn survey, 90 percent of top salespeople use social selling

- At the same time, cold calling has a success rate of a mere 2.5 percent

- More than 60 percent of sales professionals who don't use social tools miss their quotas
- Almost 55 percent of all buyers do their research by visiting social media channels

For established B2B businesses, and even those starting out, social selling on LinkedIn cannot be ignored. Attracting today's digital buyer can no longer be done with marketing brochures and cold calls alone, if at all.

The new sales model involves sharing valuable content that your buyer is interested in and, more importantly, having a direct outreach strategy on LinkedIn (The LINK Method™) for lead generation and client acquisition.

The ROI with social selling is always there when it is implemented correctly. But another huge benefit that is often not tracked in metrics is that social selling often speeds up the sales process.

I want to wrap up this book with sharing the advice of other social selling experts, so you don't have to take my word for it. These experts are all at the forefront of digital transformation, and I asked them to share two specific insights on what they believe individuals and businesses should focus on when it comes to social selling.

The two most significant themes shared throughout this book are: **building relationships** and the importance of **high-quality content**. These themes represent the shift from the old to the new sales model and the digital transformation that has evolved from it.

Figure 12.02

Interaction, along with building and nurturing relationships, is vital. No longer is it acceptable to connect with a potential client or customer on LinkedIn and immediately hit them with your sales pitch. "Go slow" is the key phrase to remember, or better yet, just follow the exact steps and timing I laid out for you in The LINK Method™. Also, remember:

- The sales dialogue needs to shift from "What can I sell you?" to "How can I help you?"

That means investing time and energy into getting to know clients and potential clients and how to serve them best and meet their needs. The old axiom that people buy from those they know and trust has never been more valid than it is today.

Content and especially video is more important than ever. Your potential buyers are online and researching before they ever speak with you. Producing quality content that will inform and educate your prospects is necessary.

Tim Hughes shared this: "There must be a clear ROI [return on investment] on any social selling project, and all companies must be able to connect activity on social media to revenue. Revenue, (not followers, SSI, etc.), is the only measure that people should be reviewing when it comes to social media and social selling."

I wholeheartedly agree that you must measure your ROI and the KPIs you want to track. In doing so, you will see what's working, what needs to be adjusted, and, maybe even more importantly, when you gain a significant ROI on the time you have invested, it will motivate you to keep executing your social selling playbook.

It is my great hope that I have shown you the power and benefit of using LinkedIn for social selling and that I have laid out steps in a way that has been easy for you to understand and follow.

I am confident that if you implement what you've learned in this book, most specifically The LINK Method™, you will see a very significant ROI—both return on investment and return on impact.

. . .

If this book has inspired you to see what's possible on LinkedIn, please suggest it to any individual or organization you know that would also benefit from it.

Your referral may help someone else, and that simple act of a referral may be another step to unlocking a profitable new relationship for yourself.

—Melonie Dodaro

ABOUT THE AUTHOR

Melonie Dodaro is a preeminent authority on social selling and LinkedIn, author of two #1 bestselling books and creator of "Cracking the LinkedIn Code 3.0" an online training and coaching program.

She helps individuals and businesses build authority, credibility, and trust, and ultimately increase sales and revenue.

Lists where Melonie appears (partial list):

- Top 100 Digital Marketers (by Brand24)

- Top 50 Sales Influencers (by Onalytica)

- Top 10 Social Media Blogs (by Social Media Examiner)

- Social Selling: Top 100 Influencers and Brands (by Onalytica)

- Top 100 Sales Influencers (by Tenfold)

- Top 100 Marketing Influencers (by Brand24)

- 10 Must Follow B2B Sales Influencers of Our Time (by Data Captive)

- 7 Twitter Accounts That Will Make You a Better Social Media Marketer (by Hootsuite)

- 25 Social Selling Gurus You Should Be Tracking (by Anders Pink)

She's received worldwide media coverage including being interviewed on ABC, Inside Edition, CBC, CTV, NY Post, The Toronto Star, Global News, The Globe and Mail, Huffington Post, The Toronto Sun, Inc. Magazine, and many more.

In addition to her books, she teaches her proprietary methods through online programs, seminars, consulting and "done-for-you" services and is a contributing author for Social Media Examiner, LinkedIn Sales Solutions Blog, LinkedIn Marketing Solutions Blog, Social Media Today, and Canadian Business Journal.

Join the Conversation:

https://TopDogSocialMedia.com

https://linkedin.com/in/MelonieDodaro

https://youtube.com/MelonieDodaroTV

https://facebook.com/MelonieDodaroOfficial

https://twitter.com/MelonieDodaro

Download the **FREE** companion workbook for THIS book at:

http://LinkedInUnlockedWorkbook.com

REFERENCES

[1] "About LinkedIn," *LinkedIn*, https://press.linkedin.com/ about-linkedin.

[2] Hootsuite & We Are Social. "Digital in 2017 Global Overview." January 24, 2017. SlideShare presentation. https://www.slide-share.net/wearesocialsg/digital-in-2017-global-overview.

[3] Gusarov, Sergey. "Social Selling Facts." January 21, 2013. SlideShare presentation. http://www.slideshare.net/sergeygusarov165/ social-selling-facts.

[4] Schaub, Kathleen. *Social Buying Meets Social Selling: How Trusted Networks Improve the Purchase Experience.* International Data Corporation, April 2014, https://business.linkedin.com/con-tent/dam/business/sales-solutions/global/en_US/c/pdfs/idc-wp-247829.pdf.

[5] Wizdo, Lori. "Myth Busting 101: Insights Into The B2B Buyer Journey." *Forrester*, May 25, 2015. *https://go.forrester.com/blogs/15-05-25-myth_busting_101_insights_intothe_b2b_buyer_journey/.*

[6] Corliss, Rebecca. "LinkedIn 277% More Effective for Lead Generation Than Facebook & Twitter." *HubSpot*, January 30, 2012. *http://blog.hubspot.com/blog/tabid/6307/bid/30030/LinkedIn-277-More-Effective-for-Lead-Generation-Than-Facebook-Twitter-New-Data.aspx.*

[7] Hisaka, Alex. "How B2B Buyers Perceive Sales Professionals." *LinkedIn Sales Blog*, September 16, 2014. *https://business.linkedin.com/sales-solutions/blog/h/how-b2b-buyers-perceive-sales-professionals.*

[8] "The rules say that we should try to repay, in kind, what another person has provided us." Cialdini, Robert. *Influence: The Psychology of Persuasion.* New York, William Morrow, 1993.

[9] Boolean searches allow you to search exact phrases as well as combine words and phrases using parentheticals and the words AND, OR, and NOT (otherwise known as Boolean operators) to limit, widen, or define your search. Collins, Jerri. "What Does Boolean Search Really Mean?" *Lifewire,* March 26, 2018, *https://www.lifewire.com/what-does-boolean-search-3481475.*

[10] Bright, Laura Frances. "Consumer Control and Customization in Online Environments: An Investigation into the Psychology of Consumer Choice and Its Impact on Media Enjoyment, Attitude, and Behavioral intention." *The University of Texas at Austin.* December 2008, https://repositories.lib.utexas.edu/bitstream/handle/2152/18054/brightl36922.pdf?sequence=2&isAllowed=y.

[11] *State of the Connected Consumer.* Salesforce, 2016, 7theraofmarketing.com/wp-content/uploads/2016/11/State-of-the-Connected-Customer.pdf.

[12] "Rethinking Retail: Insights from consumers and retailers into an omni-channel shopping experience." Infosys, 2013, https://www.infosys.com/newsroom/press-releases/Documents/genome-research-report.pdf.

[13] Hisaka, Alex. "10 Social Selling Activities Statistically Proven to Get Results." *LinkedIn Sales Blog,* May 10, 2015. *https://business.linkedin.com/sales-solutions/blog/l/10-social-selling-activities-statistically-proven-to-get-results.*

[14] Hisaka, Alex. "5 B2B Buyer Preferences to Know LinkedIn." *LinkedIn Sales Blog,* September 24, 2014. *https://business.linkedin.com/sales-solutions/blog/s/social-selling-5-b2b-buyer-preferences-to-know#%2521.*

[15] *A Guide to Marketing Genius: Content Marketing,* Demand Metric, 2015, https://www.demandmetric.com/content/content-marketing-infographic.

[16] Ku, Daniel. *The ROI Of Social Selling: 5 Data-Driven Outcomes [Infographic]*. Sales for Life, February 26, 2016, 2:22, http://www.salesforlife.com/blog/the-roi-of-social-selling-5-data-driven-outcomes-infographic.

[17] *B2B Content Marketing 2017 Benchmarks, Budgets, and Trends – North America*. Content Marketing Institute, 2017, http://contentmarketinginstitute.com/wp-content/uploads/2016/09/2017_B2B_Research_FINAL.pdf.

[18] "Three in Four Consumers Link Social Video Viewing to Purchasing Decisions." Brightcove, November 15, 2106, https://www.brightcove.com/en/company/press/three-four-consumers-link-social-video-viewing-purchasing-decisions.

[19] Beard, Randall. "Trust in Advertising – Paid, Owned and Earned." *Nielsen*, September 17, 2012, http://www.nielsen.com/us/en/insights/news/2012/trust-in-advertising--paid-owned-and-earned.html.

INDEX

Y

Made in the USA
Middletown, DE
19 December 2019